Wakefield Press

ON BEING A MINISTER

John Hill was born in the western suburbs of Sydney in 1949 and settled in South Australia in 1974. Following a career as a schoolteacher, he became ministerial assistant 1986–1989, ALP state secretary 1994–1997, and member for Kaurna 1997–2014. He held several portfolios under premiers Rann and Weatherill, most notably as Minister for Health for seven years. He did not contest the 2014 election and now serves as a director on a number of boards.

ON BEING A MINISTER
Behind the Mask

JOHN HILL

Wakefield Press

Wakefield Press
16 Rose Street
Mile End
South Australia 5031
www.wakefieldpress.com.au

First published 2016
Reprinted 2018

Copyright © John Hill, 2016

All rights reserved. This book is copyright. Apart from any fair
dealing for the purposes of private study, research, criticism
or review, as permitted under the Copyright Act, no part may
be reproduced without written permission.
Enquiries should be addressed to the publisher.

Cover designed by Liz Nicholson, designBITE
Edited by Julia Beaven, Wakefield Press
Text designed and typeset by Wakefield Press

National Library of Australia Cataloguing-in-Publication entry

Creator:	Hill, John D., 1949– , author.
Title:	On being a minister: behind the mask / John Hill.
ISBN:	978 1 74305 397 3 (paperback).
Notes:	Includes index.
Subjects:	Hill, John D., 1949– .
	Australian Labor Party. South Australian Branch.
	Politicians – South Australia – Biography.
	South Australia – Politics and government – 1990–2001.
	South Australia – Politics and government – 2001– .
Dewey Number:	324.2942307092

For Andrea,
the light on my hill

CONTENTS

Preamble	ix
Preface	xiv
1. The ministerial office	1
2. Paper	17
3. Bureaucracy	32
4. Policy	52
5. Speeches	84
6. Media	92
7. Challenges	123
8. Party	146
9. Parliament	159
10. Personal	184
Afterword	199
Thanks	202
Index	203

PREAMBLE

... the position of the Commonwealth, the federal government, has waxed; and that of the states has waned.

Sir Victor Windeyer (1900–1987) former Justice of High Court writing in 1971 on the Engineers case

I was born two weeks before the 1949 election which swept the Chifley Labor Government from power and ushered in 23 years of uninterrupted conservative rule, beginning with the second coming of Robert Menzies as prime minister.

Even by then, as a result of judicial decision-making and in particular the exigencies of war, there had been a shift in authority and power from the states to the Commonwealth. This shift, despite rhetoric from time to time about concepts such as 'new federalism', has never slowed. Indeed, the economic power of the Commonwealth, used possibly first and certainly best by the Whitlam Government to attach conditions to state grants, has bribed – some would say bullied – state governments to accept the inevitable (and reminds us of the Keating maxim 'never stand between a premier and a bucket of money'). Add to this international treaties, national codes, High Court decisions, financial bail-outs of debtor states and public opinion and it is not surprising that state Cabinets of today have less financial (and therefore policy) flexibility than ever before.

This is especially the case with South Australia. In 1901, at the time of Federation, South Australia was the third-most populous state. By the time of my birth it was number four and now, with only 7.25 per cent of the nation's population, it has fallen to number five.

So why bother? Well, even though South Australia's relative size and autonomy has declined since the Don Dunstan years, Don's utopian ideal, that dream of Camelot, is not yet dead. As Don showed, a small state can still provide national policy leadership. Indeed a smart Commonwealth would encourage it to.

When Don Dunstan became premier of South Australia in 1968 he, as a modernist and radical, changed the face of this state with his emphasis on rights, culture, lifestyle and learning. Over the next 10 to 20 years, as leaders such as Askin, Bolte, Bjelke-Peterson and Court were replaced in their states by other modernists, the agenda followed was to a large degree that set by Dunstan. Unfortunately, South Australia's modernisation was accompanied by a long hangover, the natural consequence of the bender of protectionism and state subsidy pursued by the Playford Government to create manufacturing industry in this state.

In 1974, when I moved to South Australia, all I could see was the glamour and excitement of the changes promoted by Dunstan; my father who worked as an oil executive in Sydney saw the long dark days ahead and warned me that my new state had no future. For many years, after Don had left the political stage, I thought my dad might just be right. South Australia became a state less interested in reform and more focused on survival. It was the economy, stupid! Ironically, in the early 1990s, that obsession blew up in our faces with the spectacular collapse of the State Bank and the Shakespearean fall from grace of the very honourable advocate of restraint, Premier John Bannon.

PREAMBLE

By the time of the election of the Rann Government in 2002, South Australia was in a state of depression – there was uncertainty about the future, regret about the past and cynicism about initiatives to move things forward. Mike Rann as premier, in what to his critics was dismissed as sloganeering, used to say he wanted to make Adelaide a destination, not a beloved home town. To that end he attacked the intellectual malaise that had gripped Adelaide through his introduction of programs such as Thinkers in Residence, where world-class thinkers in fields as diverse as science, design, health, film, agriculture and business came and worked, observed and recommended changes to the way we operated. He pushed his idea of Adelaide becoming a university city and brokered deals whereby a handful of international universities began operations here. He brought key business and Church leaders into the executive committee of Cabinet. And he pushed for changes in Labor's uranium policy, championed wind and solar power, and behaved in every way as the true inheritor of the Dunstan legacy. Mike's critics always underestimated his resolve.

Initiatives such as these are piddling, of course, when compared to the power of the Commonwealth Government, which as it showed during the Global Financial Crisis of 2008 is able to direct almost limitless resources and authority to deal with a crisis. It is outside of crises that the exercise of the Commonwealth's powers and prerogatives can be stifling.

Under Commonwealth–state arrangements, decisions that have the potential for cross-border effects are managed through regular ministerial conferences where the state, territory and federal ministers for a particular area come together supported by a secretariat. In practice what tends to happen is the Commonwealth outlines what it wants through a multi-lateral agreement (and what it will pay for) and then vetoes or delays what it doesn't want. At my first health ministers' conference, held, as it happened, in Adelaide in late 2005, I put the proposition that the Commonwealth Government, rather than trying to corral the states to their point of view using financial incentives, should embrace the notion of bi-lateral agreements. Tony Abbott, the then federal health minister, wasn't interested.

Some years later, when Kevin Rudd was prime minister and had put health reform on the national agenda, I put the same argument – with the same outcome.

Rudd had determined there would be national health reform involving greater national financial contributions to the states. In addition he wanted to enforce on the states a method of running hospitals using statutory boards, based on the Victorian model, where the state government appoints boards, gives them budgets, and then stands back and lets them get on with it.

While we needed and wanted the extra money, South Australia didn't want the management arrangements. Why would an administrative system developed in Victoria with a larger and more concentrated population be appropriate for South Australia? I had just implemented new legislation that allowed me to get rid of boards that hindered the progress of the development of a modern and efficient healthcare system. Be blowed if I was going to reinstate them. I made the point that Australia would be much better off if we agreed on budgets, settled on national goals, established fair ways of measuring them, and then left it up to the states to work out how to deliver against those goals. Rather than seeing the states as an impediment to national growth (as every federal politician does, regardless of party) I argued the states ought to be embraced as a means of experimentation and innovation. After all, I concluded, if the

PREAMBLE

Rudd reforms didn't work what would we do next? At least under the model I was proposing there would be alternatives.

Fortunately, we were able to avoid the worst of Rudd's plans by creating regional health boards, which he wanted, but we gave them no power. A small victory perhaps, but it showed, at least, that the mouse could still roar.

What Australia needs is a process of creative federalism that encourages bold and imaginative leaders like Dunstan and Jeff Kennett, the former premier of Victoria, to demonstrate what state governments can do, thereby creating models for the less adventurous to follow. As long as national goals are clear and budgets fair, all states should be able to learn from each other, through a process of competitive tension, about what works – and what doesn't. My views on this were reinforced by a couple of visits to Canada and in particular Montreal to visit a new hospital development. While there I became a fan of the Canadian system where the national government provides much of the health budget and sets the standards and goals and the provinces run the services, relatively unhindered. A practical example of creative federalism. Interestingly the Abbott Government's Commission of Audit Report released in May 2014, amongst its many controversial recommendations, advocated a greater role for the states in health and education and a diminished role for the Commonwealth. Maybe the time has come for the states to wax again.

PREFACE

I'll miss the House, but the House won't miss me. It never misses anybody. The House is like a sea. MPs are like little ships that sail across it and disappear over the horizon. Some of them carry a light. Others don't. That's the only difference.

Lady Astor (1879–1964), at the time of her retirement from the British House of Commons, 1945

Rob Freeman, who was chief executive of the Department of Water, Land and Biodiversity when I was Minister for Environment and Conservation, once told me about one of the National Party ministers he had worked for as a chief executive in Queensland. The MP, a National stalwart from the back blocks, had been appointed to the ministry with no policy views and little appetite for intellectual activity; in fact, without a clue about what to do. Rob, the perfect public servant, interviewed the minister about what he thought and the minister confessed he found all the laws and regulations, that he was now responsible for, complex and confusing. So Rob suggested he devote his ministry to simplifying the rules. And that's what he did, a decision that gave both the minister and the department a purpose and resulted in a significant reform of the way the laws worked – all for the overall good of the community.

You don't need to be an intellectual genius to be a successful minister.

In fact there are plenty of examples of really smart people who have come unstuck, completely, once given the levers of power. I read a very good analysis of the first Clinton presidential term that

PREFACE

demonstrated how a really smart person can get it badly wrong. Clinton, a Rhodes Scholar, a person of great intellectual capacity, was interested in everything and wanted to do everything. He wanted to be part of every decision and he found it difficult to delegate and prioritise. As a consequence his first term was short of achievement.

On the other side of politics, the far less intellectually gifted Ronald Reagan is widely considered to have been one of the most successful presidents ever. He had only three priorities: cut tax, restore American self-esteem and beat the commies. He achieved all three, while finding time to have afternoon naps.

In the Australian context Kevin Rudd, one of our smartest ever prime ministers, also suffered from an inability or unwillingness to delegate or prioritise; 24/7 Kevin just wanted to do everything. I remember during the health-reform debates, early in his first term, attending a meeting in a TAFE lecture theatre in Murray Bridge where Kevin, with overhead projector, lectured a group of about 40 people (mostly staff and media) for over an hour on the need for health reform. It was a good presentation and the people of Murray Bridge were pleased and flattered to have received their first-ever visit by a serving PM, but was it the most effective use of our PM's time?

Brainpower, or lack of it, isn't essential for success as a minister. One would hope though that a good brain well used can achieve more than a poor brain, no matter how managed.

How does one measure ministerial success? For some just getting the title, the name on the door and a bunch of public servants to do your bidding is success enough.

During my period as a minister, Caucus selected a particular candidate to the ministry who not even the most partisan Labor supporter would believe was chosen on the basis of talent.

ON BEING A MINISTER

On entering Cabinet he must have felt like Stephen Bradbury winning a gold medal when all the other competitors fell over. Sure, it's a gold medal and it can never be taken away but can it really be described as success if whenever your name is mentioned it is accompanied by sniggering.

Obviously, success means more than just achieving office. Length of tenure is another measure. Lyell McEwin was our state's longest serving health minister: he was appointed, as such, by Premier Tom Playford in 1939 and only the loss of government in 1965 – after 26 years – saw him relinquish the role. He was responsible for establishing a statewide ambulance service (St John), building The Queen Elizabeth Hospital and, of course, The Lyell McEwin Hospital.

Long tenure ensures accomplishments. But some ministers, who have had only brief tenures, have achieved a great deal too. Many will argue that Gough Whitlam was not a success; however, any fair examination of his three years in office show a staggering list of achievements that changed Australia forever: universal healthcare, fault-free divorce, the end of conscription, the recognition of China and Vietnam, and the start of a national rail system. Julia Gillard, too, during her short and very eventful term, achieved great things in education and disability care.

Obviously, achieving office and holding it for a period are essential ingredients in a successful ministerial career, but not sufficient. It's what you do with the office that's important – both in policy and political terms. Not much point in great achievements if no one agrees with you and you lose the next election and your work is dismantled.

As a political activist for over 30 years I have observed, advised, worked with and campaigned for many, many state and federal ministers, on both sides of the political divide (not the

PREFACE

campaigning, obviously). Some have been outstanding, others have been duds.

My political experience includes 15 years as a frontbencher, including almost 11 as a minister. When we stood down in January 2013, Pat Conlon and I were the only survivors of the 1997–2002 Rann shadow Cabinet. Only the premier, Jay Weatherill, remained from the Cabinet formed in 2002.

During my seven years as health minister I worked with 26 other health ministers from the Commonwealth, states and territories and, at the time of stepping down, was Australia's senior health minister. I am also the second-longest-serving health minister in the history of our state; while my position at number two will, no doubt, one day be exceeded, Lyell McEwin, the record holder at 26 years, is never going to lose his crown.

While the timing of my leaving was not exactly of my choosing, the manner was. I was prepared to have gone on a little longer, but as I had told the premier I was not contesting the 2014 election and I would go whenever he chose, I can't argue with his exercise of that option. I did not get sacked, lose at an election, get done over in a factional deal or, worst of all, resign as the result of a scandal. I went with my much greyer head held high and with positive comments from those whose opinions I respected.

I stayed a long time, left under my own steam and I think, on balance, did more good than harm. This book describes how I did the job, what worked, what didn't, and what I learnt.

1

THE MINISTERIAL OFFICE

Surround yourself with the best people you can find.
Ronald Reagan (1911–2004), 40th US President

When I worked for Greg Crafter, the Minister for Education in the second Bannon Government (1985–1989), I envisaged his ministerial office as something like a universal joint distributing the creative energy of the minister through to the axles and wheels of the department. It needed to be both flexible enough to follow the minister's ideas and wishes, and stable enough to make sure decisions were made and implemented.

Each ministerial office is a unique organisation, comprising the minister, political staffers usually chosen by word of mouth, personal knowledge, and political contacts (not the public service way), and public servants (all chosen by process – usually not on the basis of political knowledge or allegiance).

On 6 March 2002 I was appointed to the Rann Cabinet in a ceremony at Government House and given my portfolio responsibilities: 'Environment & Conservation', 'River Murray', 'Southern Suburbs', 'Gambling' and 'Assisting the Premier in the Arts' – roughly in line with my jobs in Opposition.

It was time to build an office.

I had tentatively picked a chief of staff, Kym Winter-Dewhirst, whom I had met only once.

Kym was a journalist by trade, musician by interest and a political junkie and raconteur by instinct. He had worked for a long time for the Australian Democrats at both a federal and state level, and was a passionate environmentalist who knew that territory well. He was super confident but low-key, idealistic and very amusing. I thought this combination of skills, experiences and attributes would work well for me on a professional level and more importantly I felt that we clicked and we could – as we did – build a relationship of trust. After a few years Kym was poached by Western Mining and eventually rose to a very senior position with BHP-Billiton after their takeover. At the start of 2015, Jay Weatherill appointed Kym as head of the Department of Premier and Cabinet – the state's top public servant. I had chosen well.

Before Kym could start with me, he and all other appointments had to go through a selection process run by the premier's office. Mike Rann had seen some pretty disastrous staffing appointments in earlier Labor ministries and was determined to exercise quality control.

I did have a driver appointed – Paul Adey, whom I had not met. The premier's long-term driver, Barry, decided that Paul and I would get on well and he was right. Paul was my driver for almost eleven years – I spent more time in his company than anyone else's in that time. His greatest skill wasn't his driving, his conversation or his sense of humour (all of which were outstanding) but his discretion. Paul, prior to the election, had been driver to the former Minister for the Environment, Iain Evans, who after the election became the shadow minister and my direct political opponent. In the almost eleven years we sat together, across the 400,000-plus kilometres we travelled, not once did Paul say anything about Iain – either negative or personal. In the early days I would raise his name and invite comment – but got nothing back. Perfect. A driver who gossips is a disaster.

I knew if Paul didn't gossip about Evans he wouldn't talk about me either. On various occasions when Paul was on leave I would receive services from other drivers, whose bosses were on leave or who were 'spare' drivers, allocated to all and sundry when the need arose. Some of these drivers were professional and courteous, others were self-opinionated and grumpy – all of which I could tolerate. But some were gossips and would unload easily and without invitation about their regular charges. It is fair to say that some of the people they had to drive would turn just about anyone into a telltale.

You have to be able to trust the environment of the ministerial car – often this is where important phone calls from the premier, other ministers and staff are taken. And on long trips especially, conversations with staff about the political and other issues of the day take place. In addition, of course, a ministerial driver inevitably learns about your family life. As part of my responsibilities, over all those years, my dear and long-suffering wife Andrea would often have to get dressed up, be collected by Paul to meet me in town for a dinner, ball or arts event. She and Paul would spend hours together as well – after 11 years Andrea, Paul and I had few secrets left; but they are all safe.

On that first day of ministerial life, Paul picked me up from Parliament House with Andrea, her mother Mavis Wilson, and Deb Pow my electoral officer, and we visited the ministerial office for the first time. It looked like a department store after a 24-hour sale – there wasn't much stock, certainly nothing of value, and what was there was topsy-turvy. In the middle of this was Carolyn Lee creating order. I could tell my surprise visit was unexpected and somewhat unsettling. I tried out my chair, desk and executive bathroom, had a quick look around and arranged to return the next day to meet with the chief executive of the Department of Environment and Heritage, Allan Holmes.

Allan told me he had asked Carolyn to set up the office, as she had experience working for former Liberal minister David Wotton. To his mind there was no one better at the job of office manager than Carolyn – but 'of course, Minister, you can choose whoever you wish'. I had no one better in mind and Carolyn agreed to do the job for a few months until matters settled. She was still there eleven years later. An extraordinarily gifted and hard-working manager, Carolyn worked prodigious hours, taking home a large bag of files every night ensuring the paper flow was managed perfectly.

Carolyn's greatest strength, I always thought, was her ability to pick good staff, give them the right job, train them, reward them, and let them flourish. In my entire term as minister my office worked like clockwork – it was often described as the best managed office in government. Carolyn was tough – if you didn't reach the lofty heights of expected excellence and commitment you would be moved on. She would work with someone and if they didn't click they'd be gone and a better equipped worker would appear. I came to trust Carolyn's judgement of people so completely that I would get her to help select political advisors and electoral staff.

So I had my first three staff – two former Liberal staffers and one former Democrat – none of whom I'd met more than once. It was time for a Labor activist, someone who understood the Party and who could act as my eyes and ears, important to a minister preoccupied with the 'big' job. You can easily lose contact with those who put you there.

I wasn't sure who to employ, until talking to Cathie King,

THE MINISTERIAL OFFICE

chief of staff to Pat Conlon and daughter of the legendary Len King, former chief judge of the Supreme Court and importantly Labor attorney-general under Don Dunstan. She suggested Brer Adams, a young political activist and student at Goodwood Primary School when my sons were there. I remembered Brer's campaign for student council: 'Brer for Chair'. So Brer came on board. An outstanding and gifted apparatchik, who after working for me for about six years (and having been overlooked by the factional power brokers for a federal seat) moved to Sydney where he stepped into a high-powered job in the carbon-trading section of Macquarie Bank. Brer always knew what was happening in the Party: who was up for a job, who was on the nose with the factions or the premier, which seat might be available, who was sleeping with whom. Useful information for a minister to know.

We also needed a media advisor and Kym recommended Nick Talbot, who had previously managed the newsroom for the ABC in Newcastle. He had just arrived in Adelaide with his new wife Laurel Irving, the political reporter for Channel 10. Nick was a vegan and a committed twitcher and looked about half his 40 years. With his dark-framed glasses, neat hair and square handsome face he resembled Superman's alter ego. He was incredibly energetic and in his own words 'undiscriminating' – which meant that every media enquiry was given the same treatment, including access to me, whether it was prime-time TV news, a throw-away country weekly with a circulation of 2000, or a student radio program with no audience whatsoever. It suited our purposes in those early days to be in the media a lot. I was a new minister in a new government and there was a lot of goodwill – and no one really knew me. It was a good time to be active.

The highlight of this media flurry for Kym was the morning

ON BEING A MINISTER

I featured in the first three ABC radio news stories. We became so good at getting media coverage – at least one media release a day – that Stephen Halliday, Mike Rann's chief of staff, let it be known that it wasn't a good look for the environment minister to have a media profile greater than all other ministers – including the premier! Good advice. It was only when former *Advertiser* journalist Catherine Hockley replaced Nick after two years that I realised I didn't have to talk to every journalist in South Australia whenever they wanted me; discrimination and management worked as well.

I made one other ministerial advisor appointment in 2002, a caring and smart woman who had come from the environment movement and worked for me as a volunteer in Opposition. She knew the territory, the environmental politics and all the key players. Unfortunately, it became clear relatively quickly that a political office, with its pressures and demands, wasn't her ideal working environment. It was suggested that I ask her to go and, after avoiding this for as long as I could, I did so. I didn't like it, but a boss must sometimes make these calls for the good of the organisation.

Some ministers fill a number of the public servant positions with political allies and friends, which is their right. For instance, personal assistants are often political appointments. A PA completely controls your life as a minister – makes appointments, arranges time off to see the family, schedules Party meetings, deals with the most sensitive papers including those from Cabinet. You cannot get this wrong. You have to be able to trust this person completely. For this reason I appointed Deb Pow as my PA; Deb had done an outstanding job in my electorate office (EO) and wanted to join me in the ministry. After about a year Deb decided to return to the EO and I replaced her with Yvette

THE MINISTERIAL OFFICE

Latty, a bright young woman who had worked in administration in the office. Yvette was not at all political – but a natural as a PA: highly organised, tough as old boots with those who wanted to bully their way in to meet me, fiercely protective of my privacy and space, and deeply respectful. Yvette was part of my office until my very last day as minister. In all that time she only ever called me 'Minister'. Now, I had a pretty relaxed attitude about how I was addressed; generally my staff would call me Minister in meetings and John in private, unless they were being ironic. (Kym addressed me as Minister, while making an exaggerated bow, long after he had left.)

Yvette just couldn't use my name – I pestered her at one Christmas lunch to call me John, in that environment, at least. She did so once only – and then didn't call me anything for months to come. I felt bad for teasing her and realised it's best for others to decide what they want to call you. Tony Sherbon, SA Health CE, called me John from the very first meeting; David Swan, his successor, always called me Minister, in even the most informal settings. Alex Reid, head of Arts SA, a friend as well as colleague, always called me Minister in a work setting, even if it was just the two of us. When I asked her why, she said that was the way she had been trained.

In using the title Minister, staff show respect for the office and sometimes respect for the person holding the office.

An SA state minister's office consists of around 20 or so staff: four or five political staffers (the ministerial advisors including a press secretary), 10 to 12 administrative and clerical staff, and two to four ministerial liaison officers. The last group is usually made up of professional staff from the department chosen for their skills, knowledge and contacts. They operate as a kind of transmission system ensuring the minister and department are in sync. In practice, they deal with a lot of the day-to-day issues involving constituents and MPs, seeking information, solving problems, chasing up briefings, rewriting letters, and so on. One of the longest serving in the health office was Paul Hunt. For years he was the person to whom frustrated patients, family members, the mentally unwell and threatening callers were connected in order to be calmly assisted. Every day for years, without losing his cool, while opera or classical music played quietly in the background, Paul would systematically diffuse difficult situations under both Liberal and Labor ministers.

As Chairman Deng, former leader of the Peoples Republic of China and Mao's successor put it: 'It doesn't matter whether it's a white cat or a black, I think; a cat that catches mice is a good cat.' That's how I felt about my staff – it didn't matter to me that they had worked for other political parties or weren't political themselves as long as they did their job competently and could be trusted. I did, however, like to have staff from both of the Party factions working with me.

I was one of a very small group in Caucus who was not a member of a faction. In Cabinet three of us were non-factional: Premier Mike Rann, former Adelaide lord mayor and member for Adelaide Jane Lomax-Smith, and I. All the rest were either left or right factional members. Not that factional consideration often intruded into Cabinet's decision-making processes. Once you went into that room, factional positions counted for little. It was getting into the room where the factions counted.

The left and right were allocated a number of spots based on their proportion of support in the Caucus. Mike, Jane and I were the exceptions. With the three of us now gone, there are no non-factional ministers. Following the 2014 state election there were no non-factional members of Caucus either. Not that I can claim non-factional purity; I had been a member of the Centre-Left faction, pretty well from its establishment in the early 1980s. It had been set up in order to support Bill Hayden and other like-minded independents in the federal Caucus. When the Centre Left eventually imploded under pressure from thwarted ambitions, branch stacking, bullying and a general lack of belief in anything but power, I, unlike most of its former members, didn't rush to join one of the other factions, but chose to stay unaligned.

I felt pretty secure as I had just been appointed ALP state secretary and endorsed as the candidate for Kaurna. In particular, I thought a lack of factional alignment would help me stay neutral in my position as secretary. In general terms I probably saw myself more as a left winger – particularly in terms of social policy and activism. However, I always found the left's focus on process, ideology and traditional economics somewhat dispiriting. The right's pragmatism and economic rationalism I found more appealing; however I could never abide the religious moralism applied to social issues from its dominant sub-group. The majority of the right is more pragmatic and less moralistic; and it is disappointing that many feel the need to toe the line on the social issues in order to advance.

Over my term I increasingly came to value legal skills in my office. Even though I had a law degree, I had never practised law and realised I knew just enough to be dangerous. So over the years I employed a number of people with legal skills who were very helpful dealing with Crown law, advising on the complexities of legislative drafting, defamation and industrial matters – and on the various court cases ministers become involved in.

The health portfolio is always embroiled in either an

enterprise bargaining round or an industrial dispute of some sort. Party activists Chris Picton and Aaron Hill came to my office (at different times) as law students – both very young and impossibly bright. Chris became in turn an advisor, my chief of staff, an advisor to federal health minister Nicola Roxon, and then her chief of staff when she became attorney-general – all before the age of 30. At 30 he was preselected to replace me in the seat of Kaurna, winning comfortably in 2014 and becoming the Party's youngest MP. Aaron came to me from Senator Don Farrell's office, was poached by industrial relations minister Paul Holloway, then became advisor to federal treasurer Wayne Swan before finally returning to SA to work as economics advisor to Jay Weatherill – all before he was 25!

It has often been said that successful bosses employ people who are smarter than them. If the IQs of my former staff are any indication, I was a huge success.

It is common to hear criticism of the prevalence of former staffers amongst the ranks of MPs. And it's true we wouldn't want a parliament filled by people with the same backgrounds and experiences, but surely experience, knowledge and skills obtained as a political 'apprentice' shouldn't be reviled. Why and how would a farmer, teacher or furniture manufacturer be better as a politician than someone who had spent time learning the craft? I was amused when Steven Marshall, the MP for Norwood, following his election as Opposition leader said his inexperience was a bonus because he wasn't a political hack like Jay Weatherill. What spin! How ridiculous it would sound if anyone were to apply that logic to any other role. 'My lack of experience as a surgeon/driver/furniture manufacturer is an advantage! That other guy who has spent years learning and practising his craft is just a hack!'

THE MINISTERIAL OFFICE

Of course, not all political advisors become politicians – some have no such desire and others lack the opportunities – however they all learn a huge amount, which they can then apply to whatever tangent their careers take.

Along with the lawyers I employed many journalists over the years, and not just as media advisors.

After Nick Talbot left, Catherine Hockley (who had been the *Advertiser*'s very energetic environment writer) came on board. Kym and I had got to know Catherine well – we had given her good stories, which she had covered thoroughly and fairly.

On one occasion I introduced tough legislation to deal with the construction of drains in the south-east of the state. The former government had started a multi-million dollar scheme to assist with the removal of salt from the landscape. The removal of vast numbers of trees by farmers had mobilised the huge deposits of salt, which were rising to the surface and reducing the productivity of farmland and killing native trees.

The scheme had merit but the former government, which had a lot of political support in the South East (often begrudgingly given), was reluctant to force the scheme on unwilling participants. One major landowner, Tom Brinkworth, disagreed with the government approach and built his own drains (eventually winning payments from the Libs after the event) which directed the water to where he wanted it: into large wetlands where he could indulge his passion for duck-hunting.

The scheme was a mess. So I decided to introduce legislation to allow us to finish the scheme, link all the drains and take the surface water and the salt out of the landscape. To achieve this the law needed to allow the Department of Water, Land and Biodiversity to obtain, compulsorily, the required land, without compensation and without appeal. The majority of landowners strongly supported this approach – because they knew they would be beneficiaries. Tom was not one of them. Earlier I visited Tom with my departmental officers to see if we could reach agreement. I inspected the monstrous channel he had constructed and been recompensed for and he took me on a drive around his property, as he explained his philosophy. In the cabin of his ute he had two guns: one on the tray behind the seat and one on the passenger side – in fact resting between my legs as he drove me around. Tom wasn't a subtle man. He agreed the scheme was a mess and stated the only solution was to let him finish it, his way. I said we could not have two schemes, and we weren't going to have his.

I returned to Adelaide and had the legislation drafted. Pleasingly, Rob Kerin, by then the leader of the Opposition, agreed to support the measures if I included a compensation scheme for those disadvantaged and a sunset clause to limit the number of years in which the necessary powers could be exercised. I agreed. The local MP, Mitch Williams, who had been elected as an independent and then rejoined the Libs after one term, said he couldn't support it.

The legislation was prepared and launched. Catherine Hockley, then environment reporter, called me. 'Was this an anti-Brinkworth measure?' she wanted to know. I couldn't possibly comment. Why don't you ask him? She did – I'll never forget the next morning's headline: 'Power to Take Farmers' Land "Mugabe Like"'. Brinkworth said the powers being created were 'something I would expect from President Mugabe in Zimbabwe'.

Later, as my media advisor, Catherine implemented a strategic approach to the media – I wasn't talking to every journalist whenever they wanted. My life became less frenetic. Although at first I missed it I came to realise that I didn't have to spin around

THE MINISTERIAL OFFICE

like a top to do my job. Catherine really understood and enjoyed the environment portfolio and was somewhat crestfallen when we moved to health in 2005. Nonetheless, she threw herself into it and when Chris Picton left to go to Canberra she became my chief of staff for the challenging 2010 election, when the new RAH was a major and defining issue between the two parties. Catherine and the rest of our team performed brilliantly during this period.

Once on a ministerial visit to England to look at new hospital developments, I was accompanied by both my CE Tony Sherbon and Catherine Hockley. As they were a couple by then it seemed natural they share a bedroom. After all, the taxpayers saved the cost of a room for a few nights. It wasn't until we returned to Adelaide and the Opposition, in its usual trawl for dirt and scandal, requested, through FOI, receipts from the trip that we thought anything about it. We had a bit of a nervous laugh wondering how Tony would explain the charge to his room for dry cleaning a dress. A missed Opposition goal!

Catherine married Tony and I was very sad when they eventually moved to Canberra. I admired the way they managed to separate their personal and professional lives – it must have been tough – and it was not at all surprising that after the election, which had been bruising for us all, they decided to move on.

After Catherine Hockley stepped down as media advisor the search began for a replacement. After eight years in government we had churned through much of the available talent in Adelaide and beyond. Who could I get? The health portfolio was huge and always in the news – we needed someone of exceptional skill and energy. Fortunately out of the English gloom emerged Ruth Awbery, born in London but with connections to Australia through her Australian mum and a desire to live for a time in Adelaide. Ruth had left a very successful career reporting politics for the BBC – including for a time presenting a morning radio program in London. Ruth appeared happy to go from interviewing British prime ministers to writing media releases for a minister in a small state of Australia. Ruth brought a new energy and a great sense of humour to the role.

Her usual advice to me as I went to a press conference was: 'Try not to be interesting!' – her way of trying to get me to stick to message, as I had a tendency to extemporise and reflect broadly in a teacherly sort of way during press conferences. This could mean that the story reported was not the one intended. This happened spectacularly on one occasion when my 'by the way' comments resulted in a front-page story about changes to the law around the treatment of patients as they were dying. The front page of the *Advertiser* 8 May 2009, roared 'LIVE AND LET DIE Hill urges debate over terminally ill'. The premier's office was not happy.

Inevitably, as in any office, there is staff turnover. In 11 years I had 17 or so 'political' staffers filling the five or six available slots, and many others moving through the admin or liaison positions. Generally, people left for reasons of professional advancement or to pursue a personal dream of some sort.

The week would always start with a diary meeting – involving my political staffers, speech writer and PA, and the parliamentary officer, whose job was to make sure papers for parliament, briefing notes, bill folders, and answers to questions and so on were properly arranged. These meetings allowed me to talk through the week's events and highlight potential problems. Like meeting each week with the CE, these meetings required very little organisation. Amazingly not all ministers used such structures. If you expect people to perform well they have to know what's going on.

Looking back at the kinds of people I employed it is possible to discern some patterns: with few exceptions they were journalists, lawyers and academics; all professions where analysis and language skills are paramount. All professions where precision about details, working to a deadline and strong opinions are to the fore. People who are paid to be paranoid.

Having detailed (or indeed any) knowledge of my portfolio responsibilities was an advantage, but not essential. I had departmental officers for that. Nor did I mind whether or not my political staffers were 'political' in the sense of being Party activists; though, as I mentioned before, I always found it valuable to have at least one staffer in this category. I missed this link during my last couple of years as a minister.

I also know that all my staffers had personal qualities to recommend them.

In the early days of my ministry, Kym and Brer started referring to 'Team Hill' – and during all the changes in personnel and portfolios the moniker stuck. It demonstrated affection for me, which I was grateful for, but also a pride in and loyalty to the team. This was reflected every day in the extra hours worked, the extra effort to get things right, and the celebration of every success, personal and professional. Our office had a culture built around regular morning and afternoon teas, lunches and occasional group outings and, until the very health-conscious Leah Manuel came, bowls of chocolates (usually Haigh's) left in the kitchen. Vic Rodney, a psychologist and long-term MLO (ministerial liaison officer) was a keen and excellent cook and arranged many staff cooking competitions and group lunches in our boardroom. This was a great way to get to know each other and see people performing in new ways. Many members of the 'team' were incredibly fit and ran, danced and played sport together. Kath Thomas, a nurse and weekend roadie for her son's band, managed the MLOs and was brilliant at arranging events – staff picnics, Fringe outings, and so on.

Ministerial offices can be tense places: pressure, long hours, public criticism – and in some offices when things go wrong, as they always will, the minister shouts, staff get bawled out and an oppressive environment develops. This in turn makes people scared to make mistakes or admit them, staff turnover increases, leaks occur, morale declines, and performance suffers. Avoiding this seems self-evidentiary, yet the pattern occurs over and over.

I can't say I was always successful, but I did my best as minister to create an atmosphere of openness and calmness and expected my senior staff to show similar qualities. Mistakes were identified quickly and dealt with without recrimination. Ours was an office where there was always laughter – even at times of great pressure. It was a fun place to be.

PAPER

Remove the document – and you remove the man
Mikhail Bulgakov (1891–1940),
Ukraine-born, anti-communist writer and surgeon

At the heart of my strategy for managing files is what I call my 'clean desk' strategy (and what others describe in less flattering terms).

The clean desk strategy is something I learned in 1986 while working as an advisor to Greg Crafter and with then director-general of education, John Steinle, who always had an immaculate office – no clutter, no overflowing in-tray, no piles of paper. In fact there was nothing on his desk, other than his telephone. Back then there was no computer either. Every time I went into his office, which was frequently and usually without an appointment, his desk was exactly the same: completely clear. So I asked him how he did it. No big deal really – he dealt with every bit of paper, every file as it arrived. He approved or rejected, read, filed or discarded every piece of paper every day.

This is about good decision-making: dealing with a file once and giving it, when it arrives, the level of concentration it deserves. If an 'interesting' journal article lands on your desk, decide whether or not you are going to read it; if you decide you will, then read it today – don't put it in a pile with other interesting articles for consideration later. That pile will grow and, with every addition, weigh upon you. If you are not going to read it, bin it.

In addition to moving paper on as quickly as a hot potato I also developed the habit of deleting all my email and text and recorded messages after reading or listening to them. This wasn't to get rid of incriminating evidence but flows from my strong desire for order. Life, particularly ministerial life, can be chaotic – the imposition of as much order as possible was my way of controlling the sense of panic that can flow from being out of control. Being in control, being calm, helps me think more clearly and hopefully make better decisions. Others have been unkind enough to suggest that I am somewhat obsessive-compulsive.

With this approach, I never prioritised files – I opened them in the order in which they appeared in my in-tray, focused, decided and moved on to the next one until they were all dealt with – no need to prioritise when they were all dealt with that day. If something was really urgent and had to be dealt with straight away, someone would tell me – it wouldn't be placed in the in-tray. In my 11-year career as a minister I had three offices: my electorate office, my Parliament House office and my ministerial office (where I spent most of my time). On every day of that 11-year term each of those desks was completely clear, apart from a phone and computer. The only time there were papers on my desk was when I collected them from an in-tray held by my staff. Paper discipline is at the heart of good decision-making, which is the heart of being a successful minister.

Many people claim a clean desk is a sign of a sick mind and chaos a sign of creativity; such people also often claim to be able to readily put their hand on every file. These people are fibbers. They are also deeply suspicious of those of us with mild OCD tendencies.

PAPER

When I was first a shadow minister I kept my parliamentary office in pristine condition, much to the amusement of my more creative colleagues. Close to my office was one shared by former MPs Vini Ciccarello and Lyn Breuer – to me their office resembled a set from the *Steptoe* TV series from the 1960s, containing as it did every conceivable piece of clutter: files, clothing, trophies, bottles of wine and Vini's famous bike. It was impossible to sit down as every chair was covered with junk.

One day I arrived at work to discover my own tidy office with its paperless desk had been completely turned over – there was crap everywhere. I was enraged that my sanctity had been breached and was on the verge of asking the Clerk of the House to call the police when the laughter of Vini and Lyn alerted me to their guilt. While I didn't appreciate their practical joke at the time, eventually I recognised it was a handy reminder not to take myself and my theories and habits too seriously. After this I was less free and easy with my commentary about Vini's and Lyn's office arrangements.

§

In bureaucracy a version of Newton's third law applies – every action generates an equal and opposite reaction. If you write, email or call a minister or their department, then you generate a file. An email campaign, say, to oppose changes to the way a clinical condition is managed might generate hundreds of files. One for every identical chain email. Each one of these files then comes to the minister to sign and date so the equal and opposite common response is then emailed to the individual emailers. Chain emails responding to chain emails.

An extraordinary amount of effort and cost is associated with every contact the public makes with the bureaucracy. Often those who write about government waste or poor priorities or big bureaucracies are responsible for feeding the machine they lambast.

One of the biggest, most ridiculous and futile such campaigns was mounted following the government's decision to add fluoride to Mt Gambier's water supply. Fluoride had been added to most of the state's water reticulation system progressively from 1971; by 2010, 90 per cent of our citizens had access to reticulated fluoridated water.

For technical reasons smaller communities were excluded, including the Mount. I was advised that this no longer needed to be the case, and as the kids of Mt Gambier had, according to a 2004 survey, 78 per cent more tooth decay than Adelaide children, I determined to do something about this. You would have thought this a no-brainer. And it was – except the no-brainers came out in force, making the same arguments with the same exaggerated claims that had been mounted in the '60s and '70s. They were aided and abetted by one of the strangest-ever members of the Legislative Council, The Hon Anne Bressington – a woman who came from political obscurity and received just 32 primary votes at the 2006 election. Nonetheless, she was elected for an eight-year term on the basis that the highly populist and very popular (later Senator) Nick Xenophon placed her at number two on his ticket. Nick received such a high primary vote that his surplus elected Ms Bressington, whose wacky views were brought into the Leg Co. While it is true that all but the top candidates on any Party's Legislative Council ticket receive few first preference votes, at least voters know in those cases what the candidates are standing for. This was not the case with Xenophon's running partners who all stood as 'independents'.

I'm absolutely certain the vast majority of Nick's voters would not have supported many of her views and would be horrified by the consequences of having trusted Nick's judgement in placing her as his number two. Bressington had a subsequent and very public falling out with Xenophon; gratifying but it didn't alter the fact that she was elected for an eight-year term. The anti-fluoride campaign was also supported by a number of very passionate Mt Gambier locals, including the mayor of Mt Gambier, Steve Perryman. He went on to become the Liberal candidate for the seat of Mt Gambier at the 2010 election and, I think it is fair to say, he didn't make his fluoridation views a major plank in his campaign. He lost to an independent candidate who supported fluoridation – as did the local federal MP, the state Opposition, and most rational people. This didn't stop the email and letter campaign that flooded my office; at the end of my term I was still getting anti-fluoride correspondence – from all over the world.

Conspiracy theorists love the internet and use it obsessively to promote their views. None of these letters or emails usually makes an iota of difference to the decision – but each has to be answered with all the time and expense that entails.

Nonetheless the volume of correspondence, especially when it is composed of personal letters from individuals, can be a handy way of telling whether or not a policy is on the nose. Political reality being what it is, you make a judgement reasonably swiftly that your original policy needs some degree of 'reworking' in such cases, or you hold out until the premier or Cabinet tells you to roll over.

During my term I had cause to perform more backflips than most Olympic high-board divers, achieving a magnificent '10' for my backflip over proposed changes to country health.

Any MP or public official will tell you that a relatively small number of their electors contact them with questions, comments or requests for assistance. Many ask only once, are genuine and in need and hopefully receive help. Providing assistance in such cases is about the most rewarding part of the job.

Equally, individual letters or emails to ministers about cases of genuine hardship or bureaucratic neglect or incompetence deserve to be treated seriously and if considered properly can lead to change. Greg Crafter told me he thought one of Don Dunstan's greatest strengths was his ability to make substantial reforms to the law or policy based on the issues presented by such individual cases.

On the other side of the ledger a proportion of correspondents or callers are regulars who ask petty and pedantic questions or make peculiar and often bizarre claims. Nonetheless, all of these requests have to be treated seriously too. When answers are provided, these correspondents or callers are rarely satisfied and can become more and more demanding.

This is a syndrome I am sure, particularly associated with retired men of a certain age and disposition. It's a bit like doctor shopping among those with pharmaceutical dependence or psychosomatic illnesses. This syndrome involves authority shopping – zany complaints to local councils, state MPs, federal MPs, the governor, prime minister and so on.

Then there are the individuals who pursue bizarre legal cases. I was regularly, as health minister, summonsed to court by a woman to address charges that the health system had surgically raped her and planted a transmitter in her brain. Another person rang the ministerial office pretty well daily, for months on end, threatening suicide, public scandal or worse if I didn't deal with his/her allegation that the 'system' had against his/her will forced a sex change upon him/her.

What do you do? Make a file in almost every case. Hours and

hours of valuable time and emotional energy of senior public servants, lawyers, and politicians are taken up with treating seriously each and every one of these matters. You ignore them at your peril, because every now and then the bizarre will be true. What if the cross-gender person had carried out his/her threat to self-immolate in the emergency department of one of our hospitals and we had not taken the threat seriously? The agitators of course know how the system works and it gives them huge pleasure to see the machinery of government cranking up to deal with their latest outrage.

Not all files are generated by the deranged or politically motivated; the bureaucracy itself initiates files to inform the minister. For example, the manufacturer in Victoria of a soft cheese may have recalled voluntarily that cheese from the market because listeria had been found in a number of samples. The brief might say it is unlikely to be a problem in SA because the cheese is not sold in this state. The department will inform the minister of these facts because they know there is a chance the media might hear about the Victorian case and ask the minister, in the middle of an interview about nurse numbers, say, whether or not there is a problem in SA. It's better if the minister can be definitive rather than vague on this point because the media may otherwise report that SA is also at risk resulting in panic, the disposal of perfectly good cheese, and damage to local industry. Many of these 'for information' files appear every week.

To those files can be added the files that require decisions – surprisingly few as a proportion – plus Cabinet submissions, parliamentary briefing notes, correspondence to and from colleagues and federal ministers, updates on every aspect of the department's operations including budgets, technology, building works, enterprise bargaining arrangements, national performance comparisons, and, increasingly, huge numbers of politically motivated freedom of information requests. The list goes on.

Each year at our staff Christmas lunch my chief of staff would provide the stats for the year. At the 2012 lunch my final chief, Dominic Stefanson, told us the office had processed 6215 files in calendar year 2012. I had attended 866 formal meetings and given 201 speeches. My media advisor had issued 133 press releases and my chauffeur had driven 44,645 kilometres – more than the Earth's circumference.

Each ministerial docket requires an enormous amount of work before it is presented to the minister for decision, noting or signature.

Let me give a reasonably common health example. A son writes about perceived poor treatment of his mother in one of our hospitals; he claims she waited too long for treatment and received no food, water or pain relief. When the letter or email arrives in the minister's office it is copied digitally and transferred to the department for a draft response; given that the complaint is about a third party a letter will be generated to the son with a form for his mother to sign giving him authority to access her records. After that condition is satisfied, the complaint letter will go to the relevant hospital where staff involved with the patient will be interviewed, records from the date of attendance checked, and eventually a response letter drafted. The draft will then work its way through the health system, being checked at various levels for style, grammar and spelling; and for policy, legal and insurance issues.

The letter will eventually make its way to the minister's office. Once there a ministerial advisor will give it a political once-over. That is: does it answer the question raised by the constituent, and are there any political considerations that need to be taken into account? We might want to include in the letter that while the mother may have waited longer than desired, new initiatives (e.g. an upgraded emergency department) will address the problem in the future. The letter is then formatted following a particular style guide, placed in a file and transferred to the minister for signing. The turnaround between the letter being sent and a response being signed is around six weeks.

One practice I had employed from early on was italicising the part of my letter containing a technical explanation.

I would write along these lines:

Dear Mr/Ms Patient,

Thank you for your letter about problem x; I have referred the matter to my department for an investigation and advice. The department has investigated the matter and advises me that:

Mr Patient was seen at the hospital and was treated by the attending clinicians and according to their notes all proper procedures were followed. The doctor on duty apologises to Mr/Ms Patient if the service provided was not satisfactory.

This would be followed by a final paragraph from me thanking the writer again, adding my own apology (if relevant) or adding information about policy initiatives or providing a contact if relevant.

This mechanism separated the experts' advice from the political to emphasise a proper process had been followed.

Every day the files arrive – some simple letters requiring a signature, some complex files requiring judgement and perhaps the expenditure of millions of dollars. The health department had delegated authority to spend up to $1.1 million; the minister's approval is required beyond that, up to $11 million. If more than that, Cabinet agreement is required.

Managing signing is not the sexiest topic to write about, but it is essential to running an effective ministry. As I have already mentioned in my earlier years (1986 to 1989) I had the very good fortune to work as an advisor to Greg Crafter, then Minister for Education and Aboriginal Affairs in the second Bannon government. Greg was a thoughtful, compassionate and tough-minded minister who achieved a great deal in his various portfolios. Time management, though, was not his strength; as an advisor I was forever telling him the time to let him know he had to move on to the next appointment – but he frequently became absorbed by the people or issue in front of him, to the detriment of the diary but endearing him to those he was with. Consequently, he would regularly get behind in the signing of his documents – the one area that could easily (at least in the short term) be ignored. So instead of having one case of work to deal with, by the end of the week he might have three or four bags going home with him and often returning (unopened). To remedy this he hit upon a process that took responsibility of the files away from him and shared the responsibility among his advisors. We kept the files and made times in his diary to go through them with him, making the changes required and pushing the most urgent ones. Greg mastered the discipline of files in his own way and was a success.

There is a tendency in bureaucracies to pass problems up the chain until eventually they arrive on the minister's desk. (And there is a worse tendency to sit on problems in the hope they will go away.) That allows everyone to say, 'It's on the minister's desk,' when asked where a particular file or response is at. That's not something that could have been said fairly during my 11 years.

To reinforce this I always had the in-tray placed next to my PA's desk so anyone could place in it files requiring my attention, but they wouldn't become my responsibility until I collected them. It also made it easier for staff to retrieve files that needed updating for some reason. Not that they stayed in the tray for long – during the course of the day in spare minutes between meetings I would grab a handful and deal with them. Any left over could be read and signed in the car on the 50- to 60-minute trip home. I could count on one hand the number of nights I had to take an unsigned file into the house to deal with. Weekends were different, because usually I would spend Fridays in the electorate and a bag of work as well as the Cabinet papers would be delivered to my home on Friday evening by my driver, Paul Adey.

This, I know, was not the case for all ministers. In fact on occasions when acting for other ministers on leave I was presented with bags and bags of files that they had been unable or unwilling to look at; either through fear of making a wrong decision or inertia. Sometimes it is prudent for a minister to delay in order to seek further information, but procrastination is not prudence. Generally, delay and anxious examination of options doesn't change the decision, just wastes time and causes more anxiety as the files requiring decisions pile up.

One of my colleague ministers from another state was notorious for not dealing with his files. While I was chair of the relevant national Ministerial Council, I became aware that this minister was up to a year behind his colleagues in signing off on national decisions that all other ministers had promptly agreed to. Reportedly he was a star in parliament – the Opposition could never lay a glove on him – but when it came to files he was hopeless. As it turned out he had deeper problems, announcing publicly at one stage that he needed to take leave to deal with a serious illness. The whisper was he was suffering from alcohol poisoning. He had apparently gone to a staff farewell party, collapsed in a drunken stupor on the staff member's floor, and awoken the next morning realising he had an event to attend. He went to it, made an incomprehensible speech, and then claimed illness to cover the gaffe.

This case reminded me of a now deceased Labor Speaker of the SA House of Assembly, a prominent lawyer before and after his term in parliament. He was a very intelligent man, but the stress of the Speaker's job was obviously too much for him and he took to locking himself in the Speaker's office where he got pie-eyed drinking brandy. Being drunk made him somewhat erratic but not, by any means, the worst Speaker ever seen in SA.

When dealing with a file, ministers are generally given only two options: 'For approval' or 'For noting'. Usually, this presents few problems and the file can be dealt with easily. Sometimes the file might be very long and/or complex and/or controversial and/or confusing. The human tendency in such cases is to put these files to one side and deal with the more straightforward ones. You do this for too long and you end up with a bag of very awkward files that you never want to face. In such circumstances, department officers can rightly say 'it is on the minister's desk'. Often these files represent uncertainty in the agency about how to proceed or are written by technocrats, who are superb at all aspects of their jobs other than being able to communicate in non-technical English. My standard response to these files was to write on them: 'For face-to-face briefing' or 'For discussion with CE'. This meant the file was no longer in my possession and through eventual discussion with the relevant official I would fathom my way through the issues and make an informed decision. Often the discussion was brief and the answer clear.

PAPER

I did consider anything more than a couple of pages to be overly long; my office issued general instructions that files be kept to two pages, with annexures or appendices as necessary. Travelling home at night flicking through a bag of files is always a burden but heart sickeningly so when you pull out a file of four or five – or more – pages. Strangely enough, arts officers could be quite wordy, often when dealing with relatively straightforward and simple issues. I guess they liked telling stories.

Decisions about policy are always the best to make – it's easy enough for a layperson to think through such issues. Is it a good idea to restrict smoking around children's playgrounds? Yes or no? Should we build a new RAH? Yes or no? The worst decisions are those where you are asked to sign off on expenditure to buy a piece of equipment or enter into a service contract worth millions and millions of dollars that has been subject to a tender process and evaluated by experts. In one sense it is straightforward, if the process is above board – sign. But really, as a minister, you are absolutely reliant on the officers who present the file to you. Yet decisions above a certain amount have to be agreed to by a minister – in reality, in relation to these decisions, the minister really is a rubber stamp.

As minister the biggest contract I signed, after agreement by Cabinet (and as their delegate) was for the procurement of the new Royal Adelaide Hospital – a construction price of $1.85 billion payment, which is included in the average $397 million a year we agreed to pay for a total of 30 years to cover capital, interest, maintenance and service costs. The process was as good as it could be and I was – and am – confident it was a good deal.

§

In 2010, I discovered the iPad and much of my 'paper' became digital. So my diary, my daily briefing papers, speeches, press releases, statistics files and even my Cabinet papers were all managed by one app or another. Apart from the obvious convenience it also meant the inevitable daily updates and changes could be constantly incorporated.

I thought this a great leap forward in managing my daily workload and was pretty chuffed to discover I was the first Cabinet minister in Australia to have my Cabinet documents uploaded digitally. Of course, this was accompanied by the predictable media handwringing about what would happen if I left the device on a bus, or it was stolen. By now most ministers, certainly in South Australia and I'm sure elsewhere, take it for granted their files will be accessed in this way.

While I was the first to take up this technology I can't say I really understood how any of my gadgets worked, and for my term as minister I had the luxury of staff who could fix problems for me. They would remind me of my password, make sure chargers were available, software and hardware updated, and when something went wrong they would get it fixed. Fabulous for me then. But now, without this support, I feel like Rip Van Winkle waking from a long sleep and having to learn how to do these things myself. I was telling Ruth Awbery my former media advisor about this after leaving office and she reminded me of something that caused some mirth in the office.

In 2011, I had decided to travel to England and Norway to look at some recently built big hospitals, good models for our new RAH project. Amy Kitselaar, my efficient PA, was going through the organisation of the trip with me: passports, currency, diary, European power adaptors and so on. Finally she came to a blue cloth for me to clean the iPad screen.

PAPER

'I don't need that!' I said, 'the screen's always clean.'

'Yes,' Amy replied, 'I clean it for you every morning.' A good reminder of how dependent a minister is on the hundreds of small actions by loyal and dedicated staff, who take real pride in seeing their boss well turned out.

BUREAUCRACY

> Bureaucracy is not an obstacle to democracy
> but an inevitable complement to it.
> Joseph A. Schumpeter (1883–1950), economist

It is probably not surprising that finding a positive quote about bureaucracy was a little difficult. Most published epithets are critical, though none perhaps as despairing as Franz Kafka: 'Every revolution evaporates and leaves behind only the slime of a new bureaucracy.'

Certainly many in politics adopt a sneering attitude to the bureaucracy. In fact the use of the term 'bureaucracy', with all of its pejorative connotations, is frequently used by those who want to have a go at the public service. It certainly plays well in the media; the talk-back kings and the foot-in-the-door reporters love nothing more than stories of a heartless, remote bureaucracy oppressing poor individuals.

Opposition MPs love to rail against the actions of individual public servants – while sometimes they have genuine complaints they are often exaggerated. One of my favourite MPs from the other side was long-serving country MP Graham Gunn, now retired. Graham loved nothing better than to stand up in the House and lambast the faceless 'Sir Humphries' who would stop his constituents from doing various things, often (but not in the following example) involving the destruction of large amounts of native vegetation.

This is Graham in full flight:

> *the people of South Australia are going to be interested when this government, at the behest of its Sir Humphries and bureaucrats, plunders their pockets. We are at a stage where the public has nearly had enough of this attack upon their pockets, at the behest of insensitive bureaucrats ... If the bureaucrats think that they are going to continue to get away with this, I have news for them: you are at the end of the road.*

There are plenty on my side, too, who believe bureaucrats stop the implementation of favourite policies. This is not a view I share (with the possible exception of some Treasury officials – but I'll get to that later). Jay Weatherill would often say that the 100,000 or so people who make up our government bureaucracy are our greatest resource. I agree with him. It is the engine that allows government to progress ideas into policies and policies into actions. And, like any engine, if it has a poor or inexperienced driver it won't operate well.

Each government department forms its own bureaucracy, which in turn is part of the overall government bureaucracy. Getting all the elements to operate together is a major challenge. What is clear is the various elements will never blend successfully unless the individual departments have strong and effective leadership. Each department or bureaucracy has two leaders – the minister and the chief executive. Getting this dual leadership right is a key to ministerial success. This relationship can make or break a minister; and it is a key to overall government effectiveness.

The first critical decision for every minister managing a department is to decide whether or not they can work with their chief executive; I suspect the reverse is also true. You cannot have a half-hearted relationship. As a minister you only get to hire and fire this one person – all other public servant positions are subject to a process well removed from a minister's hands. Except for the CE. So once you have chosen, you have to trust that person completely – with your goals, concerns, and challenges. While you must not politicise the position, the CE needs to know about the politics of the short and longer term and where the minister stands. Most public servants who reach the highest echelons of bureaucratic life know what is needed – the problems are caused by the raw ministers who turn up not really knowing how to relate to senior officials.

After the 2006 election Jim Birch, the then health CE, announced his resignation. Despite my entreaties to him to continue, he had had enough and after some decades in public service wanted to move on to the private sector where with less grief he could make a lot more money. Fair enough.

Recruiting a chief executive, I knew from previous experiences, can be a drawn-out process and given the relatively small size of our jurisdiction and the non-competitive salaries we offered, I was nervous about getting someone of quality who could drive the changes I thought health needed. I wanted an outsider if possible because I believed the existing relationships were a bit too cosy and they needed, I thought, a fresh set of eyes and ideas.

The appointment committee came up with a short list of recommendations. Tony Sherbon, then CE of ACT Health, was on that list but not the person the panel thought would best suit my style. They thought Tony's blunt style wouldn't gel with my more conciliatory manner. I had a different view – if the minister was to be the 'good cop', he needed a CE who could be the 'bad cop'. I had seen this when I worked for Greg Crafter, a good cop type, who recruited Ken Boston as head of education – another leader who knew how to get things done. He famously said about the education department: 'This place needs more movers and shakers and fewer movers and seconders.'

Strictly speaking, all departmental heads in SA had contracts with the premier and so it was his call. Mike Rann had fairly strong views about the recommendations and encouraged me to dig deeply. I did. In the process of making the decision I spoke to the professional recruiter, members of the interview panel, some of Tony's former work colleagues, and his former ministers. The references for Tony were outstanding – he was clearly the best candidate and Mike and I concurred that we should offer him the job, which he accepted.

Despite the appointment panel's concerns, Tony and I got on exceptionally well. A trained doctor, he was technically very skilled, as well as being decisive and exceptionally hard working. He certainly let me know if my suggestions were rubbish. I liked that because I knew it meant the ideas he didn't reject were worth pursuing. Changing a system – especially one as sensitive and complex as health – is not done easily. And it is true that while we could have done some things with more finesse, change is what I wanted and change is what I got.

After the 2010 election, Tony decided to move on – he picked up a Commonwealth position working on national reform – and so I had to recruit again. This time I didn't want a change agent – the change process had begun – rather I wanted someone who could consolidate and settle in the changes. This time an insider was the logical candidate, and I was pleased that David Swan, who had worked closely with Tony as his executive director of operations, was recommended. David was a popular choice; he understood our system inside out, knew all the players (both good and evil) and could get on with the job without wanting to throw all the cards in the air.

When Nicola Roxon first became Minister for Health (a role she went on to fill superbly) she was worried about her most senior public servant, the estimable Jane Halton, who had been CE under Tony Abbott when he was health minister. My advice to her was to get rid of Jane or get on with her – but don't try and build a system around her. I'm pleased that Nicola put aside her concerns and she and Jane went on to become a formidable combination – pushing through health reform, introducing plain packaging for cigarettes, and generally making a difference. A powerful engine with a strong, intelligent minister works every time. I have no idea what Jane Halton's politics are, they are irrelevant; she served her minister as she should in a democracy and then went into a polling booth and voted however she wished.

When we came to government in 2002 a number of CEs were moved on or moved around for various reasons. A couple of the decisions made, in my view, were wrong. Geoff Spring, brought in to run education by the Liberals, was moved on. He was disliked by the teachers' union because he was tough and was implementing the Liberal agenda, which the teachers did not much like. But he was effective – we removed him and he was followed by a few nice chaps who really never got on top of the system. I am certain that if this effective operator had been allowed to continue he would have delivered powerfully for us.

Kevin Foley, with responsibility for economic development as well as Treasury, decided the economic development agency, then known as the Department of Industry and Trade (DIT), needed new leadership and he moved its CE Jim Hallion sideways into primary industries. Jim, who had survived rough seas and overturned boats in the Sydney to Hobart yacht race, took it all in his stride. He proved a huge success and was promoted to run the massive transport and infrastructure department under Pat Conlon and then became CE of the Department of Premier and Cabinet. Kevin Foley had cause on more than one occasion to remonstrate with himself for pushing him out of DIT.

One of the agencies I inherited as minister was the small Department for Water Resources – which had been carved out of the environment department by former premier, John Olsen. We planned to abolish it, largely following the advice of the former head of environment, John Scanlon, who didn't agree with the Olsen changes and walked away from the diminished environment department without fuss or acrimony.

John recommended to us the establishment of a single department covering natural resource issues – the Department of Water, Land and Biodiversity, affectionately known as WaLaBi. I decided that it needed a new head and had the unpleasant duty of letting the Water Resources CE know he wasn't in the running. I was expecting criticism, but Iain Evans, the former environment minister and my 'shadow', let me know he agreed with the decision.

As a minister it is a comfort to know you can get rid of your chief executive if you choose. Many would argue that such a power has led to the politicisation of the public service and as a consequence a minister no longer receives frank and fearless advice from a permanent head whose obligation is to government and not the government. My experience does not support – at least in South Australia – this commonly expressed view. People good enough to become departmental heads are strong enough to express an opinion. In fact the best public servants relish the new arrangements because it means they don't have to languish in a queue waiting their turn. From a minister's point of view, while the criteria for the selection of a chief executive doesn't include political allegiance, a savvy CE will understand the political agenda and offer advice to assist ministers achieve their political goals – as it should be in a democracy.

The biggest fight Greg Crafter had as education minister (and arguably his greatest achievement) was ending the promotion by seniority system for school principals, which had for decades seen the sclerotic control of schools by like-minded males of a certain age and disposition. Following the changes and the opening up of competition there were many more women appointed to leadership positions. While a few of the dispossessed complained that schools had been taken over by the 'femocracy' (read politicised) the reality was that the quality of school leadership improved dramatically across the board.

As in schools, so in departments: permanence of position does not guarantee political neutrality. What's to stop an ideological government from promoting permanent heads with the same ideology, and who in the guise of 'fearless and frank' advice promote that ideology to successor governments of a different persuasion? Look at the history of the former head of federal Treasury John Stone who was promoted to that position by the Fraser Government, kept in place by Labor Treasurer Paul Keating, and who later went on to serve as a National Party senator for Queensland.

One CE who I did want to keep in his job was Allan Holmes, the CE of the Department of Environment and Heritage, who had been appointed from within the agency by former Liberal environment minister Iain Evans. Because of that appointment and Allan's propensity to speak his mind, there were still some in my party years later who thought him a Liberal. The worst sin. He might be – I don't know, nor do I care or think it relevant.

What I do know is that Allan was always loyal to me and the government's agenda. He would challenge and query decisions he thought wrong or short-sighted, but he would always get on with it. Sign of a good CE in my book; the worst CE, by the way, is one who agrees with everything you say. I enjoyed my relationship with Allan very much and we did achieve great things in the environment area – a clear set of election commitments, not much money, but lots of ideas and energy.

I take some responsibility for Allan's outspokenness – I encouraged him. I was old enough to remember the days of the formidable permanent heads of departments who were strong public figures in their own right and would often present publicly. The modernisation of politics following the television age made personalities out of ministers, and the limited tenure of CEs (which I support) means the nightly news is dominated by political figures. Politicians have made a rod for their own backs: by forcing ourselves into every positive story we can hardly complain when the media want us for the negative ones too. CEs have largely become backroom operators.

I was keen to do something about this and encouraged my CEs to get into the media. Allan really flourished – even highlighting his musical tastes on a regular ABC spot. My colleague Pat Conlon really understood this best of all – he'd do the media if he had to but preferred most announcements, both positive and negative, be made by Rod Hook, the head of his agency, who developed quite a prominent media profile. I think the media accepted this – because it was both good and bad news; they knew Pat wasn't hiding.

Jack Snelling, my successor as health minister, adopted a similar approach. He relies more than I on his departmental officers to deal with issues of an operational nature. It appears to be working. It is a welcome development – not every action or decision needs to be the subject of political point scoring.

Premier Weatherill, re-elected at the 2014 election, decided to exercise his prerogative and terminate the contract of Rod Hook. Rod didn't go quietly; as Tom Richardson wrote in his *InDaily* column following Hook's sacking: 'The past week has been the Festival of Rod, with seemingly every media outlet graced with his indiscreet musings on the injustice of it all.' As a result of Hook's exploitation of his profile in this way it is possible that ministers in future will be less willing to share the stage with their department heads. This would be unfortunate.

I knew I could trust Allan Holmes; as shadow minister I would seek and receive briefings and attend functions where we would meet – he was always polite and genuinely friendly but would never give away information that might damage his minister. I knew he could be trusted. On the other hand I recall, as a shadow minister, receiving a briefing from another senior public servant who proudly told me about an initiative his agency had been working on for the then minister. He even gave me a copy of the policy in draft form. I could hardly believe my luck. I took the policy, gave it a snappier title, changed it only marginally and released it during the election period before the minister could release his version. That guy was not going anywhere.

Of course many public servants are active, as is their right, in political parties, their union or around specific issues. That's fine as long as they know where and how to draw the line. What I didn't like as minister, and I am pleased to say it didn't happen very often, is that implied conspiracy that someone on your side of the political fence will assume during meetings. It always made me feel uncomfortable.

Like all relationships, that between a minister and a

department has to be nurtured. In all my portfolio areas and across my 11 years as minister I met on a regular, usually weekly, basis with my chief executives. In the case of health, a Monday morning pre-Cabinet discussion, for an hour or so, with a detailed agenda and a team of people present. At times there seemed to be more people sitting around the table than to be found at the Paris Peace Accords. I would have preferred a smaller group (and certainly had that in the environment area) but health with all its complexities required more personnel. So the CE would bring an executive assistant (to record decisions), his communications director (as so much of what we discussed had a public face) and then relevant directors responsible for items on the agenda. As the new RAH project was on the agenda each week, its director David Panter was always in attendance. On my side there would be my chief of staff, media advisor and other advisors from time to time.

The agenda would consist of standing items (New RAH, election commitments, Cabinet program, budget and so on); items placed on the agenda by me for discussion with the CE (usually big or small matters arising during the week), and items placed there by the CE (often items for ministerial decision or early warnings of potential problems). This meeting provided the backbone of the decision-making process and ensured the department and I were on the same wavelength. It was a place where my 'thought bubbles' could be 'workshopped' or 'deflated' and where departmental propositions contrary to government policy (or politically dangerous or stupid) could be killed off.

This weekly meeting created a safe place for free discussion, where both sides are able to speak their minds. It's no good where the CE takes a 'yes, minister, your wish is my command' approach. While all my CEs would let me know if they thought my ideas were crap (and, if I insisted, still do their best to implement them) Tony Sherbon, the CE with whom I had the longest association, was the most blunt. Tony never left me in doubt as to his opinions, either positive or negative. I liked and respected that.

This weekly meeting provided the structure for policy development and decision-making; and pretty well everything I did, as a minister, went through this funnel. The department's actions came to the table too, allowing all of us to operate on a 'no surprises' basis. Of course in politics, as in life, there are plenty of surprises that have to be dealt with on the run – and good staff on both sides who are familiar with the thinking and modus operandi of both minister and CE will make quick judgements about what ought to be done.

While the constructive relationship between minister and chief executive is essential for the effective implementation of government policy, it doesn't hurt if the troops get to know and see the minister too. As well as the usual introductory walk around the department when I was appointed to a portfolio, my approach, generally, was to be out and about as much as possible. As environment minister, that involved visiting parks in every corner of our state and meeting the people who run them, often sharing a meal and sometimes the ground under a tree.

One of the highlights of my time as the environment minister was travelling along hundreds of kilometres of dog fence with members of the Dog Fence Board – one of the quirkiest of all bureaucratic units – on their annual inspection. The fence is important to graziers as it keeps dingoes away from sheep; and the board members take their role very seriously. We started our trip near Fowlers Bay, at the Great Australian Bight, where the fence begins and continued at what seemed a snail's pace as the convoy of four-wheel drives stopped frequently to test and fix sections of the fence, some of which was held together with wire from the 1940s. Other sections had been electrified; and one of the members of the board, a big solid bloke, would test the strength of the voltage by holding the electrified wire in his bare dinner-plate-sized hands.

The system for maintaining the voltage was an example of outback ingenuity. The power was generated by small solar panels and stored in car batteries placed in old domestic fridges for protection against the elements. I noticed the fridges were padlocked and was told this recent innovation was to combat local Aboriginal drivers swapping their dud batteries from their clapped-out cars for the freshly charged and new batteries. Another example of outback ingenuity.

At night we made camp and a gourmet meal was prepared for us and for locals from surrounding stations. Plenty of red meat, red wine and red-blooded company. For vegan Nick Talbot, my media advisor, the trip was a mixed blessing – as a twitcher there were many bird species to spot, but special provision had to be made for his meals.

As health minister I liked to visit hospitals and talk to staff about the reform process at various stages of its implementation – these were often tense affairs that excited interest. While I didn't necessarily convince everyone (or indeed anyone it seemed on occasions) of the merits of the reform process, at least they heard what it meant for their site; and they got to hear about it from the minister and the chief executive in person and could put questions and options we would do our best to address. Hopefully it also helped develop the understanding that the individual sites were part of a much bigger system.

I also liked to visit the wards and specialist areas and talk to staff about their work. I usually came away from these visits energised, full of ideas and just enough new knowledge to make me dangerous. I liked to see how machines worked, hear how drugs performed, or learn about new surgical procedures. I especially enjoyed visiting laboratories and talking with researchers about their work.

We have internationally significant research happening in this state, which few people know anything about. One of my proudest achievements is the development of the South Australian Health and Medical Research Institute (SAHMRI), located in its architecturally impressive building alongside the New RAH. I believe this will be transformative for our city and expose more of our citizens to the wonderful work done by our very gifted researchers – bureaucrats in white coats!

When I first became health minister our health and medical researchers were in the doldrums. Their facilities were poor and their share of the national research budget was in serious decline. The central problem seemed to be one of scale – many small research institutes competing with one another as well as much bigger institutes in other states. The solution to their problems was not clear. Then I got talking to local stockbroker Alan Young at a fundraising dinner for the Flinders Medical Centre Foundation, which he chaired. He was well on his way to compiling a multi-million-dollar fund to build the now completed Flinders Centre for Innovation in Cancer. When he took over as chair, he told me, he had moved the organisation to look beyond raffles and morning teas to be more professional and ambitious. This unplanned discussion suggested a way for us to proceed. So, following Tony Sherbon's advice, we commissioned Alan together with John Shine, the then head of the phenomenally successful Garvan Institute in Sydney, to make recommendations about research in South Australia.

Their report, the Shine-Young Report, recommended the consolidation of the best of the research effort into one institute, bringing our three universities together as collaborators rather than competitors, with SA Health as a partner. They also recommended a flagship building to house the research hub. We calculated the cost at about $200 million. We had no money – but we had a plan and cooperation (eventually) around that plan – then the GFC and the Rudd Government's stimulus money came and allowed us to catapult our research community into the vanguard of international research.

It is important for public servants – the bureaucrats – to have a minister who cares about what work they do, understands it to a degree, and who defends them from unfair attack. I always felt supported as a minister by my public servants – they always gave to me what I tried to give to them: loyalty and trust. On many occasions both inside and outside parliament I had to defend senior public officials, who because of their positions were unable to defend themselves. Perhaps it was because I had once worked as a public servant, but I was always happy to do this and was rewarded with virtually leak-free departments.

Here are some typical Opposition comments about my most senior 'bureaucrats':

On 17 June 2008 Isobel Redmond commented: 'Of course, Tony Sherbon has been brought into this bureaucracy from interstate specifically to be a knife man for the government.'

On 24 July 2008, Graham Gunn had this to say about David Panter: 'The bloke with the earrings and one or two others in the Health Commission wrote it [the country health plan] ... I say that the minister ought to take a look at this character: it would instil him with confidence! [Irony I think] These people have set out to rough up and viciously attack country people ...'

On 23 September 2008 Vickie Chapman said: 'Dr Sherbon, Dr Panter, all the head honchos in the Department of Health want absolute control.'

Chapman, again, on 18 February 2009: 'How many times have people come in from England or New Zealand to tell us what is world-class, best practice, the greatest model? There have been plenty of them. We had that, I remember from Dr David Panter in the department over country health, and what a disaster that was! He has now been put in charge of the Marj/Royal Adelaide Hospital rebuild, so I hate to think where we are going with that.'

What strikes me from rereading these criticisms is how parochial they are, and how personal. They are also politically quite stupid: there are about 100,000 public servants in our state – they all have families and they all vote. Why alienate such an important sector of the community? And how can an Opposition member with these views then move into a ministerial position and work with the public servants so reviled? It amuses me how easily our 'conservative' MPs break conventions such as the independence of the public service whenever it pleases them.

I mentioned above that I didn't agree with colleagues who believed the bureaucracy tries to stop the implementation of government policy – with the possible exception of Treasury. Undeniably, it is the role of Treasury to implement the government's overall budget policy – i.e. we shouldn't spend more money than we have. The treasurer and Treasury bureaucrats often have to push that policy in the face of a dozen or more ministers pushing other policy agendas – a difficult and unenviable task. Incidentally, I never could understand why so many ministers wanted the role – a sense of power perhaps?

There seems to be a general approach taken by Treasury to any policy initiative that requires money:

1. It's not really needed,
2. it probably won't work, and
3. if you have to do it, take it out of existing allocations.

Probably not a bad set of hurdles for a minister to jump over – a minister should be able to prove the need, effectiveness and necessity for new money. But even when those criteria had been addressed to the satisfaction of everyone else, there were often, annoyingly, times when Treasury would still play 'Dr No'.

One case towards the end of my term as health minister demonstrates the case. When I took over as minister for mental health, SA Health was about halfway through implementing the *Stepping Up* report recommendations – a $300 million dollar investment in new facilities; and more importantly a new approach to treating mental illness, involving a greater emphasis on prevention and early intervention – the 'steps'. The plan involved moving some of the resources invested in traditional hospital-based care into other facilities – not without its critics, but pretty sensible and generally supported by the mental health community. One glaring omission from this set of recommendations was in the area of forensic mental health. Our forensic beds – 40 in all – were spread between James Nash House at Oakden, where there were 30 beds constructed in the 1980s in a then (but no longer) state-of-the-art facility and 10 beds on the Glenside site, which were to be abolished and placed on the James Nash site in a budgeted $19 million extension.

The trouble with this strategy was that 40 beds were not enough – all the experts said we needed about 60, given our population. Fortunately, we were are able to use some Commonwealth money to construct 10 sub-acute beds – a kind of much needed halfway house – for forensic patients on the James Nash site. This still left us 10 beds short. I asked the department if we couldn't use the budgeted $19 million more creatively – and they examined, on my urging, the possible use of converted shipping containers, as used very effectively in some mining communities and prisons; they were no cheaper. We also looked at converting other facilities – also without success.

Finally, Brendon Hewitt, SA Health's competent and pragmatic assets manager, realised that with some simple tweaking the new 10-bed $19 million facility could be extended to become a 20-bed facility – at an extra cost of between two and three million dollars. A lot of the cost of the new facility was security (a big wall!), which could just as easily serve 20 as 10, and with some minor extensions to shared facilities the extra spaces could be created. But we had to act quickly – the parliament's Public Works Committee had already signed off on the arrangements and if we didn't make the change now the opportunity would be lost – we would be short 10 beds and face, presumably, another $19 million investment in the future when the pressures became so great that extra beds couldn't be avoided.

Realising we had checked off the first two Treasury questions (Is it needed? Will it work?), we considered the third: Can we pay for it out of existing allocations? The answer was yes. Under-expenditure in another capital line gave us the available money and it seemed the needed recurrent costs should be readily available because the forensic patients who would use those beds were already somewhere in the system. They were either in other mental health beds or in prison facilities, soaking up the extra costs in those locations, especially in ad hoc security arrangements.

Taking these patients out of mainstream acute mental health beds would also take pressure off emergency departments by freeing up beds for mental health patients who could sometimes wait a long time in emergency departments. This was a 'win win' if ever I saw one. Nevertheless, Treasury fought it every step of the way. The extra capital should be used for other cost pressures; the recurrent costs weren't covered; we may not need those beds in the future; and so on. The same predictable responses. At this point I completely lost confidence in the capacity of Treasury to deal creatively and positively with health. That hadn't always been the case.

When the proposition was brought forward to build the New RAH, Jim Wright, the former CE of Treasury, offered positive solutions and suggestions. He also asked the hard questions – but got the importance of the project and understood the long-term financial as well as health advantages.

The Global Financial Crisis meant an end to that collaborative and creative approach. Post GFC, governments faced terrible choices and the pressure on Treasury officials and treasurers must have been enormous. Somewhere along that track two agendas appeared: the government's agenda and the Treasury agenda, with, seemingly, Treasury working actively against government policy.

Over many years the government had campaigned on expanding elective surgery in our hospitals and making sure that at the end of each financial year there were no overdue patients – a huge turn around and something Labor could be very proud of. In my last year or so as minister it was regularly put to me and health that we should ease off on this campaign and settle for something closer to the national average. While I accepted that our state's health budget – like every other state health budget – was growing faster than our revenue base I would never accept that the way to reduce costs was by reducing access for the sick.

The only long-term effective strategy to reduce spending

is through improving general community health, thereby reducing the need for hospitalisation. We also need to use the existing resources more efficiently, for example by reducing duplication and by having senior doctors available at all times and not pay through the nose for them to come in after hours. All of these strategies were being pursued – none was politically easy or short-term and all required up-front additional expenditure; but the long-term benefits will be a healthier community and an affordable healthcare system.

I was delighted, therefore, when Jay Weatherill in the lead-up to the 2014 election decided to include Treasury in his responsibilities – a great burden and no doubt a huge personal sacrifice. But no government can have two agendas. Treasury had to be brought to heel. It was a necessary and, as it turned out, successful short-term strategy to maximise our chances at the election. Following that success Weatherill decided to divest himself of all other responsibilities, including Treasury, no doubt believing that in a hung parliament all his energies needed to be concentrated on the big picture.

§

Every area of government responsibility has to deal with more than one bureaucracy; as well as the public service there are unions, advocacy groups, statutory officers, professional associations, charities, not-for-profits, businesses, consumer groups, service clubs and so on. A wise minister maintains good relations with as many of these organisations as possible. A lot of my time each month involved meeting with representatives of these groups. Just about all of them wanted a regular cycle of meetings – usually between two and four a year. Some more, some less.

As health minister I made a point, right from the start, to meet on a monthly basis with the president and other representatives of the Australian Medical Association – one month at their office in North Adelaide, the next month at my office in Hindmarsh Square. This proved to be an important key in dealing with what satirist Max Gillies described as the 'Painters and Doctors Union'. The AMA is one of the most powerful organisations in Australia, and generally critical of government actions, especially those of Labor governments.

Before I became health minister the then president, Chris Cain, an orthopaedic surgeon, had a public falling out with my predecessor. I determined to heal the relationship. As a result of regular meetings, open and respectful discussions, and by adopting some AMA recommendations, I achieved far more than I could have ever expected. The AMA rated Labor policy at the 2006 state election more highly than that of the Liberals. After the election the shadow minister Vickie Chapman could hardly contain her fury, describing Chris Cain as 'useless as tits on a bull'. The response of Mukesh Haikerwal, the national president of the AMA, is worth recording: he said of Chapman that she did not know her 'arse from her elbow'.

POLICY

If the staff lack policy guidance against which to test decisions, their decisions will be random.

Donald Rumsfeld (1932–), US Secretary of Defense

In my early 20s when I was, to use the language of the day, 'out of it' for a longish period (coinciding with the time taken to obtain an arts degree) I had an epiphany. I realised what ailed me was not existential angst, the war in Vietnam, or the lack of an active love life; rather, I realised, I was bored. This realisation led to a feeling of euphoria – here I was a healthy, bright, well-educated, Australian citizen given enormous opportunities as a result of the luck of time, class, sex and nationality. My epiphany made me realise that tethered to that luck came responsibility: to do as much as I could with my talents and skills to make the world a better place. Pretty typical '70s hippy philosophy. But that idealism has stayed with me throughout my life and guided my career. At the reception held for my farewell from the ministry I commented that my idealism was as strong now, if not stronger, than it had been in my 20s – now, it was burnished by experience.

From that idealistic impulse my interest in policy grew. What does make the world a better place?

Jay Weatherill used to comment that when we began as Cabinet ministers in 2002 I had the drop on a lot of our colleagues in terms of initiatives for the new government to consider. The reason for this was that I had used my four years in Opposition as shadow minister for the environment to talk, read, visit and develop policy.

By the time of the election I had put together a detailed set of initiatives that an incoming Labor Government would implement to foster environmental protection. If there had been an issue, I had developed a policy to cover it. And I made sure the policies were approved by the shadow Cabinet and announced during the election. So, not only did I have a set of policies – I had a mandate! I know it frustrated some of my colleagues, especially those responsible for the economic areas of government, when I'd come to Cabinet with some initiative or other which impinged on their territory and claim the sanctity of mandate.

In the early days the mining minister Paul Holloway and I were regularly in dispute over which areas of our state should be protected from mining and which areas could be mined. Eventually, we reached an accord based on compromise – as always, the irreplaceable tool of politics. A tool that infuriates the purists, on both sides of a debate, who are disappointed inevitably when their advocate agrees to something less than their ideal.

Mike Rann ran Cabinet in such a way that not once, that I can recall, was a vote taken. If there were strong differences of opinions, as there had been with Holloway and me, generally Mike would defer until a consensus of sorts was reached. On rare occasions where this was not possible he would decide and even if the decision was against you, you would cop it, grateful in a way that a decision had been made and you could move on.

This was obviously not an approach Mike's compatriot, Margaret Thatcher, employed. Her comment on consensus: 'The process of abandoning all beliefs, principles, values, and policies in search of something in which no one believes, but to which no one objects; the process of avoiding the very issues that have to be solved, merely because you cannot get agreement on the way ahead. What great cause would have been fought and won under the banner: "I stand for consensus"?'

Democratic government for one.

Though I do agree with the point made by Chris Picton, my successor as member for Kaurna, in his first speech to parliament. Chris, reflecting on his work as a staffer to Nicola Roxon and to me on the big controversial issues of plain packaging for tobacco and the New RAH project, had this to say:

> *While there are some times when it is important to reach consensus or compromise, there are some policies, ideas and programs that are worth fighting for in their original, unblemished form ... It is often healthy to debate and pursue unequivocally matters that benefit the vast majority of people rather than seek solutions to keep vested interests quiet.*

While I was busy writing policy in Opposition, my more muscular colleagues, members like Kevin Foley and Pat Conlon, were off destroying the then government with blistering attacks based on forensic-like investigations – creating the opportunity for me and others to implement policy. One area of policy especially well developed was our initiative to introduce natural resource legislation. The legislation was designed to integrate, on the ground, the management of our natural resources.

I determined, following much discussion in Opposition, that there should be seven natural resource management boards based on water catchment boundaries, with members appointed by government on the basis of skill.

A public servant was appointed to do the detailed work on this complex piece of legislation. I gave him the general brief and

POLICY

made it clear the boundaries would be based on water catchment areas. This was important – because I knew if there was ambiguity about boundaries the issue would never be resolved. Some local government authorities were already arguing that in order to aid administrative convenience their boundaries should be used. So I told them to get the boards in place on the natural boundaries for water and changes would be made afterward, by agreement.

You can imagine my reaction when, after working on the project for a while, the appointed public servant came back to give me a briefing with a document based on totally different boundaries. Rob Freeman, the CE who attended the briefing, turned to his colleague after he had the benefit of my reaction, and said: 'Who elected you?'

The public servant involved got the message and went on to do an excellent job preparing the brief for the parliamentary draughtsman. Rob, like all good CEs, understood that the elected official, right or wrong, is the boss and if you don't like his or her policy you need to get a job elsewhere. If you want to implement your own policy – then stand for election.

Ministers are responsible for policy. It's what they are there for; it's the most interesting and creative part of the job, the part that gets you up in the morning, and makes the battles in the media and parliament worthwhile. Yet strangely enough some who become ministers aren't terribly interested in policy, as long as they get to drive in the big car and have enough people around to call them 'Minister'.

The implementation of policy, however, is the job of the agency. And no matter how attached the minister is to a particular initiative it is important to step back and let the agency do its job. That's how Reagan did it: get good people around you, delegate authority, and don't interfere unless they deviate from policy.

Amazingly, not all who achieve ministerial office cotton on to this simple and effective formula. Mike Rann railed against ministers who put their political hats on bureaucratic pegs and acted like CEs by getting involved in the minutiae of departmental operations. One former colleague, responsible for a very big department, on one occasion removed ministerial delegation for expenditure authority on amounts above $1000. This just about brought the agency to a standstill – virtually nothing could be bought, no contracts signed, no maintenance undertaken without the minister's direct approval. Meanwhile, the big questions of public policy were left unattended. And that meant political judgement wasn't being exercised.

I remember reading an apocryphal story about Reagan involving a lion who had a choice between eating mice or antelopes. On the one hand there were lots of mice about and they were easy to catch; the few antelopes were hard to catch. A lion relying on a diet of mice, however, would soon die – because the energy gained from eating mice was less than that expended in catching and digesting them. The lion choosing the more difficult task of catching antelope would flourish. Reagan only ever hunted antelope.

In 2005, the government was travelling well – except in the health portfolio. Lea Stevens, who had been minister since the 2002 election and shadow minister since 1994, was clearly struggling – both in the media and in parliament. She was up against the Opposition's most experienced and energetic spokesman: Dean Brown, a former premier and Minister for Health. He was on the attack in parliament and regularly in the media. Lea, who had started her political career with great promise, was no longer able to cut through. Perhaps a little more than ten years was too long in the job for Lea. Sadly, shortly afterwards, she was forced to stand down from the ministry altogether because of her own poor health.

When I eventually stood down as minister I had been health minister for seven years; I think now, probably too long; and like Lea towards the end I was no longer cutting through. All portfolio areas benefit from change after a time – it's a matter of judgement how long that ought to be, but five or six years is probably long enough. On the other hand, no portfolio benefits from rapid change – it makes it almost impossible to develop and implement a consistent policy agenda. Unfortunately, some areas of government have a lot of ministerial changes; this is especially true of the more junior portfolios, those first-rung jobs for new ministers, who cut their teeth and move on. While I probably could have asked for and received a change of job after the 2010 election I wanted to stay with health to make sure many of the complex policy measures I had worked hard on were allowed to become entrenched. This was especially true in relation to the New RAH, the contract for which was still unsigned.

In 2005, I had been in environment for eight years – half in Opposition and half in government and I did want a change. So I approached Kevin Foley (who was acting premier at the time) and suggested I become health minister. When Mike Rann returned it was agreed; and on 4 November I was sworn in at Government House. As Mike Rann was fond of saying, I was the first person ever to request the job of health minister. My undertaking to him and Kevin Foley was to implement the policy prescriptions needed to sort out health, absorb whatever pain was coming my way, and then not stand at the 2010 election. It didn't quite work out that way – but more on that later.

My first job as health minister was to develop a policy to deal with the enormous growth in demand being experienced by health – the annual growth in service demand was around five per cent and the annual growth in budget was close to nine per cent.

This was unsustainable. Treasury was able to tell me that at that rate of growth and with a predicted long-term revenue growth of only about half that (i.e. 4.5 per cent) the health portfolio would grow from about 28 per cent of the state budget to consume it completely by 2032. This fact became the key part of my 'narrative', policymaking and activity over the next seven years. It will be the key driver for state governments right across Australia until the middle part of the century when the impact of the baby boomer generation will have passed.

The other key stats that I used to tell the story of health were these: it was estimated in 2006 that by 2016 the state's annual population would be growing by four per cent; but only by one per cent amongst those under 14 – i.e. those who will do the work and pay taxes in the future – and by a whopping nine per cent a year among those over 75, those who will need lots of health services in the future and who won't be paying much tax. And what we also know is that an average person over 65 is twice as likely to need a hospital bed in the course of a year as someone under that age; a person over 85 is five times more likely to need a bed than someone under 65. So the predicted high growth in the number of older citizens foretold huge growth in hospital care. And it will only get worse before it gets better.

During the 2002 state election we promised that, if elected, we would undertake a Generational Health Review – a comprehensive once-in-a-lifetime look at how our system was working, what the issues were, and what actions should be taken by government. John Menadue, who had undertaken a similar review for the NSW Government, undertook the review. John was a former advisor to Gough Whitlam, head of the Department of Prime Minister and Cabinet under both Whitlam and Malcolm Fraser, and a South Australian by birth, with broad experience in business, media and public life.

The Generational Health Review found that our system was fractured, over-governed, with both service duplications and gaps, and was overly focused on acute care at the expense of prevention and sub-acute care. To use a favourite health cliché: we invested too heavily in ambulances at the bottom of the cliff, when we should have been building fences at the top.

This was a good and necessary conversation starter for reform – but it was not a reform strategy. It contained no detailed recommendations about what had to be done.

There is a big difference between policymaking in Opposition and government. In Opposition you have few resources – but lots of time. Wise Oppositions use that time to reflect, connect and prepare – as did Mike Rann. After eight years in Opposition we came to government with a detailed program and great energy. At the end of our first term we were able to run a re-election campaign on the back of the implementation of that program: 'Rann Gets Results'. In government you have a lot of resources and less time. And a lot more process.

On becoming health minister in 2005, I told Jim Birch, then chief executive, and a very knowledgeable, long-term health bureaucrat who knew our system well, that I wanted a specific plan to deal with the issues raised by Menadue, which we could implement in South Australia to make our system sustainable.

The detailed work was led by two outstanding public servants: Jenny Richter, later a deputy CE of SA Health, and Dr David Panter, later CE of the Central Adelaide Local Health Network.

In 2007, the SA Health Care Plan (2007–2016) was published.

It was a detailed road map for reform, including major upgrades of our key hospitals – including the New RAH – better coordination, more primary health care services, more elective surgery, less pressure on emergency departments and improved chronic disease management. The timing – three years before the next state election – theoretically meant that we could bed the changes down before having to face the voters again.

I now had a detailed policy document to run with; it was controversial, but it was well reasoned, logical and when fully implemented will go a long way to dealing with demand pressures and costs.

I was grateful that key individuals including Dr Chris Cain, president of the AMA, and Mel Mansell, editor of the *Advertiser*, were supportive, because there were plenty who took pot shots. Usually, along the lines of 'this policy is good overall but not the bit that affects me'.

The plan detailed dramatic changes – the most dramatic of all being the proposal to abandon the existing Royal Adelaide Hospital site and start again with a new hospital – to be called the Marjorie Jackson-Nelson Hospital – on old railway land at the western end of North Terrace. The then Opposition leader, Martin Hamilton-Smith, initially supported the proposal but then back-flipped, arguing the site should be used for a football stadium and entertainment district instead. This created a key issue for the 2010 election campaign.

The change in name seemed to excite much of the opposition to the project, especially among clinicians working in the RAH. I had decided we needed a new name because of concern put to me that the clinicians at the Queen Elizabeth Hospital would object strongly to having some of their key services, including kidney transplantation and intensive care, transferred to the RAH.

The QEH had always seen itself as a rival to the RAH, in terms of services, research and teaching, and objected fiercely to any change that might be interpreted as a downgrade. The fact that the state neither needed nor could afford the QEH to have these ambitions was of no relevance. A new name for the new hospital was seen as a way the two institutions could come together on neutral territory.

Unfortunately, I didn't foresee the reaction this would generate at the RAH and in the broader community. Western Australia had gone through a similar process and decided their new hospital would be named after a leading doctor: Fiona Stanley. I nominated Marjorie Jackson-Nelson in honour of our much-loved governor; a former Olympic champion and long-term hospital volunteer fundraiser for the Peter Nelson Leukaemia Foundation, formed to honour her late husband. 'Marj', as the governor was known, graciously agreed and then had to endure a couple of years of savage and personal abuse from those who objected to both the name and the changes.

Cabinet would have stuck to its guns on the issue, but eventually Marj put us all out of our misery when she withdrew permission to use her name. Restoring the name Royal Adelaide Hospital made it easier to talk about the project, especially with the staff at the RAH and, in the end, nobody at the QEH seemed to care one way or the other.

I am deeply sorry about what we put Marj through and will never forgive those whose nastiness was directed at her rather than me or the government for the decisions made. Vickie Chapman, the then health spokesperson for the Liberals, said (among her many criticisms) the name Marjorie Jackson-Nelson Hospital wouldn't work because it was too long. That allowed me the rejoinder that then Opposition leader Martin Hamilton-Smith couldn't make it as premier for the same reason. Vickie and other critics relished in calling the hospital the 'Marj Mahal' – a clever political tag, but a deeply offensive and personal jibe at our governor made by those who traditionally love to associate themselves with Establishment causes.

There were some in my Party, in the lead up to the 2010 election, who wanted us to abandon the New RAH project, so successful had the 'anti' campaigners been. Our research showed that the 'anti' sentiment was especially strong among the people most likely to use it – older women. Somehow or other that generation had bought the line that it was too good for them – shared rooms and shared toilets in 50-year-old buildings were all they needed.

Fortunately, the 'abandon' option was dismissed – if we had abandoned the project we would have been seen to be abandoning our principles (the hospital was needed!) and we would have been portrayed, rightly, as gutless, shameless and panicked. Further, history would have judged us poorly – because eventually the RAH would fail: basic infrastructure would break down; its inefficiencies because of ad hoc design decisions made over several generations would make it more and more expensive to staff; and it could never be expanded because of the limited site. Eventually, just like the equally criticised tram extension, everyone will think it fantastic; it will become a matter of state pride. Because of the strident opposition, everyone will remember it was a Labor initiative and that will go to our long-time future political credit.

It's easy to be a critic – a government proposes a project, in this case a new hospital, a complex decision, with multiple dimensions, the reality of which won't be seen for years – in this case, almost ten years between announcement and delivery. All the critic needs to do is raise fears: it will cost too much, we can't afford it. It's built on a fault line, lives will be at risk. It's in a flight path, helicopters won't be able to land; the land is polluted, toxic fumes will make people sick, it's too big, it's too small, it's too far from the med school, there's not enough parking, there will be fewer outpatient services, single rooms will be more expensive to staff, there are no offices for doctors and, the most bizarre of all, from then leader of the Opposition Isobel Redmond: there will be no obstetric services (true – but there are none now either – that's what the Women's and Children's Hospital is for). All of these complaints/criticisms were made and they are all without merit. Unfortunately, by the time one marshals the complex set of facts to deal with any one of these claims the critics have moved on to the next fear. Sadly, that's the nature of political discourse.

The net impact of these politically motivated claims was to sour community opinion – we weren't winning the debates over the back fence. The most powerful way of affecting public opinion is through word-of-mouth, the original social medium. The fears generated by the Liberals, given authority by some senior and more conservative doctors, and supported by elements in the media, meant people saw the smoke of controversy and assumed there must be the fire of disaster. Over recent years we have seen this technique perfected in the demolition jobs done against federal Labor over the school building program, NBN rollout, the mining tax, and carbon pricing. Critics will say the government in all those cases brought it on themselves. That's true to a degree, but it doesn't justify the extremist reactions – that can only be justified by the old political maxim: that the means justify the ends, or 'whatever it takes' – as it was put by Graham Richardson. In the case of the New RAH – the end goal for the SA Liberals was not a better hospital but a change of government.

Our handling of the issue could have been better – a lot better. We should not have dropped the idea on people without building the case for change. In doing this we grossly underestimated the real and deep-seated professional and community emotional connection to a site where many had worked, been saved, or where loved ones had died.

We should have begun by publishing a discussion paper about problems with the existing site, proposed ideas, and allowed clinicians to lead the debate about the options and trusted them to back the best. This error was compounded by deciding to scrap the name Royal Adelaide Hospital. This gave our political opponents a huge platform on which to build their case to save the RAH. Finally, I think our advertising in support of the changes, as good as it was, may have been counterproductive. It merely served to remind people we were doing something they didn't like, and that we were spending their money to tell them. This was an example of an approach famously characterised by Jay Weatherill as 'announce and defend' politics.

This alternative approach, 'debate and decide', appears to be working. Since my departure from the ministry, the government announced that consideration was being given to collocating the Women's and Children's Hospital with the New RAH – something advocated by the AMA and key doctors at the Women's and Children's. Rather than announce the decision and then defend it, Minister Snelling put it out for consultation and after several months was able to announce overwhelming professional and public support for the idea. Combining the two hospitals on the new site was part of the original Health Care Plan – but insufficient funds and my own nervousness about closing not one but two icon institutions meant it wasn't pursued.

A few years ago, I travelled to Canada with David Panter,

the gifted former British National Health official and clinical psychologist responsible for overseeing the planning of the New RAH project. We went to Montreal to learn about the development there of a similarly sized new hospital, also being built on former railway land, a year ahead of our project in the design and procurement process. Amazingly enough, in the past fifty years only a handful of hospitals the size and complexity of the New RAH have been built from scratch.

I met the Quebec health minister who told me his project had also been controversial, for much the same reasons as ours. I asked him what he had done to deal with this negativity. In SA we had tried advertising, lots of media, community meetings and so on. What had they done in Montreal? Simple, he told me with a Gallic shrug, 'I don't talk about it.' He just got on with it. After returning to Adelaide that became my default position. Stop trying to convince people, just get on with it and wait for public opinion to shift.

We were told on a visit to inspect a new hospital development in Trondheim Norway that the local paper had run the headline: 'The Hospital No One Wants'.

About a year before the 2010 state election the *Sunday Mail* splashed with a story about the creation of the Save the RAH campaign, which it continued to support strongly over the months leading up to the election. This was disappointing; the *Sunday Mail*, under the editorship of Phil Gardiner, had strongly endorsed the New RAH. The position reversed with the appointment of his successor, Megan Lloyd.

The Save the RAH team was led by plastic surgeon and part-time RAH employee Jim Katsaros, and consisted of a bunch of mostly Liberal members and fellow travellers, including long-term Liberal donor Rob Gerard. His credibility on this issue was immediately blown out of the water when I was able to reveal he had previously approached the government with the proposition we build the New RAH on his then 'on the market' Clipsal site at Bowden. Many of the others were, as I described them (perhaps unwisely, but certainly accurately), either retired or part-timers. They were old-school RAH doctors, some of whom had worked at the hospital during its rebuilding in the 1960s and were long retired. Others were visiting medical specialists – doctors who do most of their work in private practice and work usually one or two days a week in public hospitals.

I did meet and attempt to explain the merits of the new hospital to many of our opponents, including Save the RAH members, without much success, and to be fair to them they were strongly emotionally and professionally attached to the facilities and culture of the place and were grieving over its proposed demise. What they saw as the pinnacle of medical excellence in this state was being pulled down by a politician relying on bureaucratic advice. He even wanted to get rid of its name!

The campaign was very active, seemed to spend a fair bit of money, worked hand in glove with the Liberals, disrupted our campaign events, and ran candidates in the upper house and in key lower house seats. Its advocates received great media coverage in their criticisms, particularly in relation to areas where they had no specialist knowledge such as financing, the use of public–private partnerships, flight paths, soil contamination, geology and so on; factual information by departmental experts addressing their claims was dismissed or ignored. I can imagine the media outrage if the reverse had occurred and our engineers told the doctor-critics how to perform surgery.

One of the sad elements in the whole process was how the voices of those doctors supporting the New RAH were discounted or drowned out in both the media and their own professional organisation, the AMA. Rather than deal with the issue internally and come to a definitive position, based on analysis, the AMA sat on the fence – unwilling to stare down its older, more conservative members to support the workforce of the future. But, as mentioned, once the contract was signed they were quick to demand the relocation of the Women's and Children's Hospital to the same site.

Ultimately the campaign was a failure and Labor narrowly held on to office. Despite a profile any political candidate could only dream of, Katsaros received less than one per cent of the vote when he stood for an upper house position, an humiliating result.

Despite all the energy, campaign time and media attention, by 2016 Adelaide will have a new hospital at the heart of a world-class health precinct which will be the pride of South Australia. If we debated before deciding, nothing may have happened. I'm one for spending political capital – we had lots after the 2006 election and if we spent a big chunk of it on building a new hospital, then I think history will approve. Colleagues who lost seats and margins in 2010 may have a different view.

Building the New RAH, as controversial as it was, was only one element of our 2007–2016 health strategy. That strategy saw the redevelopment, to some extent, of all city and several country hospitals, and the development of a number of GP Plus Healthcare Centres to provide better access to primary health care and reduce pressure on emergency departments. That was the good news. The bad news involved reducing duplication and changing hospital profiles.

The hardest task was to bring together the two kidney transplant services (QEH and RAH) into one service, which according to the strategy's detailed service plan was to be at the RAH. The nurses and patients, especially, were opposed – as was the Opposition (naturally). All sorts of dire outcomes were predicted, but after extensive and thoughtful work the two services came together to produce one larger service. Eventually the noise died down and it worked. Interestingly, one of the most vocal critics was a nurse from the QEH who was also an active nurses' union member. I felt real delight when at the 2012 nurses' union Christmas drinks this nurse told me how well the new service was going, and that we were right to bring the two services together.

Ministers have to exercise policy leadership knowing that sometimes, in the short term, decisions won't be popular or even understood. But there is one short-term advantage of a policy framework, even an unpopular one: it can be used to address almost any criticism made about the current system.

When the Opposition raised an operational issue in parliament, say someone not being able to access a bed, or waiting too long in an emergency department or picking up a superbug, I would be able to answer along the lines: 'That's why we are building a new hospital.' Or, 'That's why we are making the tough decisions to ensure our system is sustainable.' Without that policy framework you are flying blind and every issue takes on a momentum of its own. A strategic plan or policy framework (whatever it is called) allows for the development of a strong narrative – an essential element in political discourse. This is particularly true in health where the numerous day-to-day issues can suck the minister without a plan into a vortex of mini crises.

One plan, the Country Health Plan, published a year after the Health Care Plan, didn't work in this way. At its heart was the reallocation of resources from smaller hospitals, where a majority of beds were empty most of the time, to larger centres. We planned to increase activity and create general hospitals equal in scale to a smaller city hospital like the Modbury Hospital servicing the north-eastern suburbs of Adelaide.

This sensible plan, supported by some brave country medicos, was rejected out-of-hand by everyone else: country doctors, country nurses, country media, country people and large sections of the city, led of course by the Liberal Party, whose base was galvanised. Large rallies were held across the country and on the steps of parliament. The government was accused of ripping the guts out of country communities – of being callously indifferent to the needs of country people. The logic of the plan – more services to more people more quickly – just didn't cut through, even in the bigger communities, which were particularly advantaged by the proposals.

We advertised, I toured country communities to explain the plans, answered question after question in parliament and did countless media interviews. It just didn't matter. Eventually the government and premier had had enough and I was recalled, ironically from Coober Pedy, to be with the premier when he, in an exclusive interview, gave the backflip to Greg Kelton from the *Advertiser*, where it splashed the next day.

For me this is a conundrum at the heart of modern politics and explored very well in Jonathan Green's book, *The Year My Politics Broke*, about the Rudd/Gillard/Abbott tussles: Why isn't good policy also good politics? As a politician I have always worked on the principle that if you get the policies right the politics will follow. In the case of our country health plan the policy was largely correct, but the politics were wrong.

Once again we didn't communicate the case for change very

well, and the process seemed rushed. I should have been out there a year or so earlier talking with communities about the problems of attracting staff, the dangers of running low-volume services, the cost to taxpayers of keeping open unused beds. And I should have presented options and invited submissions; I should have adopted Jay's 'debate and decide' – rather than the 'announce and defend' – approach. A better approach would have involved a trial in a willing community supported by incentives. My successor in health, Jack Snelling, has learned the lesson and I congratulate him and his department on the superb consultative process used to roll out his Transforming Health plan.

Another element we got wrong was our city-focused misunderstanding of country behaviour. We had believed country patients would prefer, if they had to travel for a hospital admission, to attend a beefed-up country hospital closer to home rather than a hospital in Adelaide. Not so. Quite reasonably, many country people said that if they couldn't use a hospital in their own community they would rather go to a hospital in Adelaide where they had family or friends to offer support. I explained this option was still available but they were so angry they had stopped listening.

However, I don't think it would have mattered how we approached the issue – the reaction would have been the same. Many country communities have seen the removal of banks, businesses, churches, railway stations and schools – their hospital in many ways is their last symbol of hope. Their attitude is easy to understand: it doesn't really matter if the town down the road gets a better hospital if my town is worse off.

If we had been more 'political' we would have allowed, by stealth, the slow erosion of services in the smaller hospitals – something that had been happening anyway for years, under

POLICY

both sides of politics. Easier to explain the closure of a birthing service here or a surgical service there on a case-by-case basis than present a root and branch restructure. Cynical but pragmatic. I'm glad we didn't do this.

The reality is, the health of country people is worse than of city people: country people are more likely to smoke, be overweight and suffer from a wide range of chronic conditions. Many country communities, even ones with hospitals, find it difficult to recruit and retain doctors and other healthcare professionals. Much of the available resource is used keeping open wards with no patients and operating theatres with few procedures, and paying doctors extraordinary sums of money to be available 'in case'. Our country healthcare plan was designed to address these issues; to address the country health 'crisis'. Unfortunately, the policy wasn't seen as a solution to a crisis; rather if there was a crisis it was created by the policy.

I should have learned from this experience. However, following the 2010 election and in a tough budget environment, Cabinet accepted my recommendations to reduce subsidies to three country hospitals, non-government-run community hospitals. One of these, the Keith Hospital, mounted a monstrous campaign to overturn the proposed funding cut. A classic case of the mouse that roared. My department's advice was that the hospital's management could be improved and that a new management with a clearer set of goals would be able to operate the hospital within the budget provided. However, there is logic and there is politics. The hospital board may not have been brilliant at management – but they sure knew how to play politics. In the end, far too much of my time for two years was taken up dealing with an issue worth only a few hundred thousand dollars to a budget of over $4 billion. A clear case of hunting mice rather than antelope.

The disappointing side effect of these country campaigns was that our huge improvements in country services – more doctors and nurses, more mental health care, more elective surgery and more dialysis – were completely overlooked. I am sure that most country people still believe the wicked Labor Government savaged country health services during my tenure.

§

In modern democracies there is a tension between the view that 'stakeholders' (that dreadful catch-all phrase that sweeps up all individuals and groups who might conceivably have an interest in a particular initiative) should be involved in some way in decision-making and the view that government should be decisive.

John McTernan, one of our thinkers in residence, was helpful in resolving that tension. He told Cabinet that stakeholder engagement should be about consent for a government to make a decision, not support for the decision to be made, welcome though that might be. I like this distinction because it makes clear what the nature of stakeholder consultation should be, while preserving the right and authority of government to decide.

One way for governments to involve those with an interest is to round up all the 'stakeholders' and appoint them to advisory bodies or committees, where they can usefully contribute to policy development or oversee its implementation in some way. An excellent example of that in action was the work done in SA Health by the clinical networks of clinicians, administrators, advocates, and patients. Carefully chosen individuals were brought together to review plans across a range of services such as cancer care, heart care, and aged services. The groups were appointed with particular tasks in mind and were not responsible

POLICY

for budgets or day-to-day delivery – but they were very effective in the delivery of improved system-wide services.

The other way for government to involve 'stakeholders' is to appoint them to boards, which in turn run services. This works in some areas of government. In my experience the boards appointed to run arts companies, for example, like the opera or Festival Centre, worked pretty well, but those elected to run hospitals, especially those in the country, were highly problematic.

In 2006, the entire health system in SA was managed through boards – metro-regional boards, individual country-hospital boards as well as country regional boards, the dental services board, the ambulance board, and so on.

Theoretically, the Health Commission (a three person board) ran the department but this had been neutered years before by the minister of the day nominating the departmental CE and other top officials to the three positions. All of these boards made central planning and coordination difficult, complex and expensive – but at least in relation to the city and service boards there was some quality control, as government generally appointed the members. One exception was the ambulance board, which included elected members and representatives from the union. Even the secretary of the ambulance union thought this wrong and advocated for the removal of the board.

But the biggest difficulties were in the country, where the 40-plus boards were elected by local communities. Members were public-spirited individuals in the most part, often local business people, including those with an interest in health such as undertakers and doctors' spouses. They often included, as every elected body does, political activists – those who like to be on boards and those who use them as springboards. Most individual boards were not expert in the running of hospitals, but were very good at defending the status quo while advocating for more resources. Just about every hospital I visited had a plan to increase the size and expand in-service delivery. Few had a system-wide point of view.

Consequently, each board had its own systems for finance, clinical governance, procurement, recruitment, industrial relations, and contract negotiations. Some would argue that getting the decision-making back to the grassroots level produces efficient outcomes and local ownership. Reality does not support this. While some local hospitals worked very well, as a result of good managers and strong board members, this was not universal. Often the boards had a hands-off approach – they were unpaid volunteers who came together once a month and relied on the competence of a general manager, who was answerable only to the board, and in many cases led the board on key decisions. If the manager was of good quality, there would be no problems, but where the board had a light touch and the manager was of mediocre talent anything could happen.

The Mt Gambier and Districts Hospital had been a problem for years, going back to Dean Brown's term as health minister. There seemed to be unresolved and intractable conflicts involving doctors, the board and management. Just before I announced plans to remove boards, I discovered the manager of the hospital, without the knowledge of his board, had through secret negotiations over the hospital's imaging contract come close to causing the existing contractor to remove services from the hospital and set up a separate in-town service. It is unlikely any other supplier would have set up in the hospital, meaning hospital patients, often the sickest people, would have to be transferred to the town centre for services. Costly and risky. Fortunately, with only days of the contract remaining, my office was informed, and we intervened to renew the contract.

There was also evidence of hospitals advertising for staff, poaching from a neighbour, which would then advertise and cause further poaching; all at great expense. We even heard of one hospital where the manager took a trip to the US to recruit staff.

There were other examples of poor financial and contract management. These and other cases convinced me to act and do what the health department had believed was desirable for years but thought would never happen: get rid of boards and run an integrated healthcare system.

The former Liberal health minister, Michael Armitage, had tried to deal with the issue with legislation, but was unable to convince his own party. He wanted to replace individual country hospital boards with a handful of country regional boards – he ended up with both.

Unlike my management of the New RAH and country health service changes I was sensible and called together representatives of the various country boards, put the case for change and, while I was not able to convince them all, I had enough support to develop a legislative strategy to get rid of all boards. Instead I created Health Advisory Councils (HACs), especially in the country. These could advise management, develop long-term plans, own property (very important in country towns where the hospitals were often established by local effort) and raise funds. I also included a provision for local MPs and local government to have representatives on the HACs.

On reflection, I am certain I used the 'debate and decide' model in this case because I knew I had to introduce legislation in order to implement the proposals – this was not the case with the New

RAH. In order to have legislation passed I needed the support of at least the majority of the Legislative Council crossbenchers and to get their support I needed reasonable support from amongst the country board members affected.

The *Health Care Act* passed the parliament in 2008, paving the way for the modernisation of the management of health in SA by allowing the development of statewide financial, clinical, procurement, contract and recruitment systems. This has led to a reduction in management positions, better accountability, massive capital works investment, fairer contracts for doctors, and a huge increase in services (elective, mental health, chemotherapy and dental) – all of which would have been impossible under previous arrangements.

§

An important aspect of our Health Care Plan was the focus on prevention. We knew we had to take urgent action on the incredible growth in obesity in our community. I was keen to have a comprehensive approach and was impressed by the French program EPODE (*Ensemble, Prévenons l'Obésité des Enfants*), which we eventually adapted to South Australia conditions as OPAL (Obesity Prevention and Lifestyle).

EPODE was a program developed by Dr Jean-Michel Borys, an endocrinologist in a working-class community north of Paris who became concerned by the incidence of heart disease among his patients and decided to do something about it. Following a long process of trial and error he started having success with a social-change-focused approach, involving children, family, school, community and local government. His data suggested it made a difference to the level of childhood obesity in the communities where it was implemented. The only other successful approach I became aware of was that used in Singapore where overweight and obese children were identified at school and placed on a special diet and exercise regime. While this approach might work in the more authoritarian Singapore I doubted it would work in Australia.

After meeting with Jean-Michel and seeing EPODE in operation in France I became an enthusiast and invited him to South Australia to explore the options for its introduction here. Jean-Michel, a former conservative local government councillor, told me that bi-partisanship was an important part of the deal. He also argued it was important to involve industry – thus, somewhat controversially, a number of food companies, including Nestlé, were sponsors. Sponsorship was necessary as EPODE's approach was promoted, organised and implemented without government grants. But for philosophical reasons as well, Jean-Michel argued all the players had to be involved in the process of change. Certainly sponsorship did not mean policy control or advertising rights.

To promote bi-partisanship I arranged for Jean-Michel to make a presentation in Parliament House and to meet MPs from all sides of politics. Jean-Michel dutifully outlined his approach, shared evidence of the program's success and invited questions. I was pleased that the Liberal Isobel Redmond, then shadow Minister for Ageing, attended and seemed genuinely interested. Eventually, she went to Paris to see the program in action for herself. Her colleague, the education shadow minister, David Pisoni, however, took a highly critical approach focusing on the industry connections. Consequently, this attempt to develop a bi-partisan approach in the state parliament to an issue of pressing public concern was unsuccessful. Nonetheless, OPAL is now up and running in communities in 18 local government areas, and making a difference to the lives of children and their families all over the state. Pleasingly, on the ground, a number of local mayors with connections to the Liberal Party have been highly supportive.

The visit to a community to see EPODE in action was one of the strangest in my ministerial life. Along with staffers Brer and Catherine, I travelled with Jean-Michel and his team to the working-class town of Beauvais, where we met the local mayor, had an interview with the local media (in translation), and met the local doctor and others involved in the program. About halfway through the visit the ever-vigilant Brer pointed out the half dozen or so casually dressed fit young people who were shadowing my every move. I had failed to notice I had been given a security detail that in Australia would probably be larger than that given to a head of state. Generally, state ministers are treated politely wherever they travel, but usually without fanfare. In keeping with the tone of the day the visit concluded with a four-course meal in a local restaurant, hosted by the mayor.

§

I also shared responsibility for the arts. When he became premier, Mike Rann made me his assistant arts minister. It made sense: in terms of status and access to budget it is good for the arts to have the premier as minister; but of course premiers are not as available as other ministers and that's where I could help. I looked after about half the organisations that made up the portfolio, attended as many events as possible and generally supported Mike as much as I could. What made it easy was that Mike and I had fairly similar views about how to run the portfolio.

While I was pleased to have been made arts minister in my own right when Jay Weatherill took over as premier, I was more pleased that on my departure (and on my urging) Jay added the arts portfolio to his many responsibilities, with Chloe Fox as minister assisting. It is also good for the premier, especially a Labor premier, to be arts minister – it gives them good access to many in the business community who support the arts through sponsorship, patronage and attendance. After carrying the huge workload of premier, treasurer and arts, Jay decided after the 2014 election to reallocate his other duties, including the arts, to other ministers.

Arts policy making is a little different to that of other areas of government. Essentially the arts community looks for three things from their minister: appreciation through attendance and regular meetings, financial support, and non-interference. A minister who goes to lots of shows and defends budgets and artistic integrity will be a success.

The last of these functions can be the most problematic. As arts minister I variously had to defend the expenditure of public money on the creation of the film *Snowtown*, which detailed the horrific mass murders in that town's 'bodies in the barrel' case; the hanging of a realistic-looking horse carcass in the Art Gallery; and an exhibition of the plaster casts of various vaginas. It can be difficult when, as always, there is pressure on health and education budgets to explain such works – or indeed any expenditure on the arts.

Funding for individual artists and projects is done through what are known as peer-based assessment processes; people in the field judge applications. This creates an arms-length approach, and keeps the politics out of it. Once you set up such a system you have to go with it – otherwise you will be accused of interfering; not that it stops unsuccessful companies and artists appealing to ministers to intervene and restore funding that has been removed. The only occasion I did feel like interfering was early on when I had to sign off on a recommendation to fund an artist to fly to Tokyo to take a series of Polaroid photographs and then to New York to exhibit them.

Richard Florida, a notable American cultural thinker and writer who came to Adelaide a number of years ago, impressed me with his analysis of successful cities and that analysis helped me justify arts spending and expression. Through his research, Florida found that successful cities were those tolerant of gays and people from diverse backgrounds; they were cities where the arts and sport were valued and ideas could flourish. The reason was simple: these are the sorts of places where bright people with energy and money want to live and invest. So while the arts have merit in and of themselves they are also an essential element in creating economic investment and growth.

The main area where Mike and I affected policy was in the expansion of festivals. We do festivals better than anywhere else in Australia – our car number plates even once tagged us the 'Festival state' – so it made logical sense to support this area. Over our term WomAdelaide, the Fringe and the Festival itself all became annual events – to the consternation of critics who predicted failure at every extension. By 2012, in raw numbers, more people attended festivals in South Australia than any other state. We even supported a festivals coordination body, Festivals Adelaide, which estimated that in 2012 'our' ten festivals provided an economic benefit to the state of $62.9 million. What can't easily be calculated is the benefit to state pride, vibrancy and the attraction and retention of young people. Flinders University academic Dr Steve Brown tried. He led a team that calculated the 'cultural value' of the 2013 Adelaide Festival to be $85 million, compared to its economic benefit of $25 million.

POLICY

We also created the Regional Centre of Culture, based on the European City of Culture concept. It came out of a discussion I had with Robyn Archer who in 2004 was engaged to direct the City of Culture project for Liverpool in England. I was inspired by her plans and thought a regional version on a much smaller scale would work. So at the 2006 state election we committed to a biennial regional centre of culture, with Port Augusta to be the first. The idea was to provide about $750,000 for programming over the course of the year and about half a million for a legacy arts project for the community.

Predictably, the mayor of Port Augusta, the late Joy Baluch, attacked the idea – she wanted the funds spent on some other pet project. But to be fair to her, once the money was spent and fantastic arts facilities were created out of old stables and court facilities, she was a fan. But the really wonderful part of the year was the arts content, including inspiring collaborations between local artists and professionals. A highlight was the opening night performance involving dozens of local guitarists performing 'Smoke on the Water' on the city's very long jetty.

The arts program over the year focused on including and celebrating Aboriginal culture; important in a community with a history of strong racial tensions. This arts program was helping build cohesion and strengthen identity, as well as giving country people access to offerings that those living in cities take for granted. Watching the Adelaide Symphony Orchestra perform on the Port Augusta golf course in front of 5000 people – many of whom had not seen an orchestra before – filled me with pride. For many of the performers Port Augusta was an unknown quantity, existing only in their imaginations based on the 'red-neck' image projected by the mayor. Many were surprised by the real beauty of the location, buildings and people. The festival brought change on many fronts and the legacy arts facilities continue to contribute to the town's vitality – including hosting the now annual Desert Fringe.

When the Regional Centre of Culture was announced as part of our 2006 election commitments, Treasury decided this was a four-year rather than ongoing commitment. Unfortunately, neither Mike nor I picked this up and while we were able to squeeze out enough money for a third festival the budget had run out. Arts SA prepared a budget submission for ongoing funding, but given the Global Financial Crisis I wasn't optimistic. What really stuck in my craw, though, was the fact that at the budget committee, which I was unable to attend, the proposition of extension was dismissed following the contribution of a former colleague who had been to one event and thought it poorly attended and that we were wasting our money. Good policy is not always self-evident.

§

Policy development usually involves much thinking, planning, discussing and consulting; but not always. When I was environment minister, the Democrats or the Greens called for a 20-cent levy to be placed on single-use plastic bags; an initiative already happening in Ireland. The bags, while useful for lining kitchen bins, were a disaster environmentally – billions escaped and could be seen all over the place in trees, caught up against fences and, of course, in the ocean where they were sometimes consumed by marine mammals confusing them for food. The media asked my office for my response.

Typically, in such a situation, a minister would put out a statement saying – 'interesting idea, we will look into it', or dismiss it as impractical. My reaction was, 'Yes, these bags

POLICY

are awful, but a levy doesn't go far enough. Let's ban them altogether!' That's what I said and that's what we did – two or three environment ministers later. After trying as hard as possible to persuade other state and federal ministers to join us, SA remains the only Australian jurisdiction to have banned single-use plastic shopping bags. Despite the anticipated backlash predicted by a number of Cabinet colleagues the policy has been very well supported. A Newspoll commissioned in 2006 by Clean Up Australia found that at 91 per cent South Australians led the nation in supporting a ban on plastic bags. It is estimated that since the ban came in 400 million bags each year have been avoided in our state (off set to a minor degree by purchased bin liners).

5
SPEECHES

Live an active life among people who are doing worthwhile things, keep eyes and ears and mind and heart open to absorb truth, and then tell of the things you know, as if you know them. The world will listen, for the world loves nothing so much as real life.

Dale Carnegie (1888–1955), *The Art of Public Speaking*

The first speech I can recall making was given in about 1965; the occasion was, I think, Anzac Day and the speech had been written by my English teacher, Mr (Evan) Sutton, who nominated me to make it to the 1000 students and 100 staff of Asquith Boys' High School. It was a somewhat daunting occasion, though the circumstances were close to ideal: I was elevated on a rostrum with a lectern for my notes and a microphone.

Essentially my job was to read someone else's words with as much energy and feeling as I could muster. While I was nervous beforehand, I felt elation after. I realised I liked reading aloud, I liked using a microphone and I especially liked the sound of my own voice reverberating back at me. In those days my ambition was to be a radio announcer, so making the speech helped flame that desire. Apart from the odd stumble I thought it had gone pretty well. Mr Sutton commented that I read it too quickly: a criticism made frequently over the years.

For a very shy person (as I was then) making speeches can be quite traumatic. Glossophobia is the technical term for those who suffer severely from the fear of public speaking and research apparently shows that a huge percentage of people would rather do almost anything, including die, than make a speech. According to Glossophobia.com Jerry Seinfeld joked that at a funeral most people would rather be lying in the casket than delivering the eulogy.

I was very shy and I am lucky that the primary and secondary schools I attended forced and encouraged me to debate, act and give speeches. These experiences didn't rid me of my essential shyness but they did give me sufficient confidence to talk publicly. Public speaking like anything else gets easier with practice.

In my early days of speech making at union or Party meetings I tried too hard, spoke too loudly and far too quickly, and acted like I was Churchill defending Britain. I was modelling myself on the master speakers of my childhood – speakers who had developed their skills addressing large gatherings often with little amplification. With the intimacy and ubiquity of television that style of speaking is now rarely heard. The new masters are speakers like Reagan and Clinton who, although they might be addressing millions, give the impression they are speaking directly to you. It's an easy conversational style. Barak Obama can do it too, but he has something else as well – his voice and oratory can move people in a way that few politicians have in the past 50 years.

By the time I had become a shadow minister I was used to making speeches and had developed a more relaxed, conversational style; though by this time rather than reading someone else's words, they were mine. On becoming a minister this had to change of course – the number and nature of speeches I was obliged to make as well as all the other responsibilities I assumed were such that there was no longer room for the indulgence of speechwriting. James Button deals with this well in *Speechless*, his account of working as a speechwriter for Kevin

ON BEING A MINISTER

Rudd. Rudd as prime minister, by Button's account, liked to write his own speeches and would often work on them until two or three in the morning. Sometimes he hit the mark, as he clearly did with his 'Apology' speech, but too often his speeches were rambling and longwinded; to be expected when the author had so many other responsibilities.

As a minister it is hard to let go of the things you once took for granted: privacy, anonymity, and control over your diary. Losing speechwriting, in comparison, was easy. When I first started, my speeches were generated departmentally and then worked on by the relevant political advisor. The speeches varied in quality enormously. When I became health minister we realised that these ad hoc arrangements were not good enough and we created a speechwriting position in the office. The position was held mainly by a former journalist, Rachel Rodda, who had a voracious appetite for obscure and bizarre facts: ideal qualities for a speechwriter in my opinion.

I liked to give speeches based on facts and stats. How many gigalitres of water did NSW take out of the River Murray every year? How many native species had we lost in SA? How many patients a year attended our emergency departments? What percentage of our kids was overweight or obese?

I also found that personal references seemed to give my speeches more credibility and allowed me to make better connections with the audience. Over the years I exploited all members of my family. In speeches to veterans' organisations I would talk about my father who had served in the Middle East and returned home quite changed. He had become a heavy smoker and drinker, always angry and emotionally closed. On only one occasion did he talk to me about his war experiences, just before he died aged 59. I am pretty sure he suffered from post-traumatic stress disorder. And I know that whenever I talked to vets they would nod their heads knowingly when I recounted his history.

When talking about ageing and health I would refer to my now 98-year-old mother, who had a hip replacement at 90 and still lives in the family home. I talked about my sons, my wife, her family and, of course, myself. Nothing can amplify a big idea like a small personal reference.

I hated giving speeches that recited lists of government achievements, made obvious political points, were full of jargon or long and boring. Sadly, I gave a few like that. Sometimes, the busyness of life meant that I'd only review the speech in the car on the way to delivering it. By then it was too late to make significant changes.

In my 11 years as a minister I gave thousands of speeches. A handful every week. Sometimes several on the one day. I can recall very few of these speeches and I'm sure I am not alone in that. Most of my speeches were fairly run-of-the-mill accounts given at fairly run-of-the-mill events. They were given at events such as conference openings, or award presentations or charity balls: events inherently worthwhile but usually not groundbreaking or of much interest to anyone beyond the audience attending.

It has always surprised me that given the general contempt the public seems to have for politicians, how many event organisers want a politician to speak at their ceremony. But invariably you are given very special treatment and made to feel honoured.

Just before the 2010 state election, Andrea and I attended the Flinders Medical Foundation Annual Ball as guests of the chair, Alan Young. He and I met at the first such ball I had attended several years earlier and we had formed a close bond and worked together on a number of projects, including the Flinders Centre for Cancer Innovation. He was grateful I had been able to arrange for the final millions required to get the Centre off the ground. I was pleased to help – the project was a good one. Alan decided I deserved special recognition and, while on this occasion I wasn't a speaker, he asked the audience of 800 or so mostly Liberal-voting business people and medical professionals to stand and give me a 'standing ovation'. He sincerely wanted to thank me but I don't think the then leader of the Opposition, Isobel Redmond, who was in attendance, especially enjoyed it. But Alan would have done the same for her if she had been in government and helped his project.

Often at such events, especially medical conferences, say about stroke or cancer, my speech would normally be fairly technical and would outline issues of relevance and detail government programs in place. I would often comment in the speech that what I was saying was better known and understood by the audience than by me the speaker – a case of taking coals to Newcastle – but the act of preparing and reading the speech helped educate me about their issues. And that had to be a good thing.

Years ago I read an essay about speech making that made the point that the speaker, in the content, style and length of their speech, shows either respect or contempt for their audience. If you are too brief or breezy or underprepared at a serious conference the audience will be offended. It would be a bit like turning up to a wedding or funeral unshaven and in jeans and T-shirt. It's why as a minister I generally wore a suit and tie. I might have been the only person in the room so-dressed, but it was to show respect, to honour the event and the people at it.

That's not to say all speeches had to be serious and formal. As arts minister I gave many speeches at the launch of programs, festivals and exhibitions. On these occasions, where alcohol was served and people were in a mood to be entertained, my speeches could be a lot looser. I especially liked Fringe and Cabaret launches – the audiences were the most ready to giggle. A 'dad joke', which would only score a groan at home, could bring the house down. Happy audiences want to laugh and it's great fun to accommodate them. Mostly on these occasions Rachel and I would include a few jokes in my speech notes. But I usually found the best jokes came to me on my feet, while the audience was laughing at the prepared gags. When people are laughing it's not that hard to keep them going.

Paul Keating, without a script, was the best political speaker I've witnessed. He could turn even the driest subject, the country's financial outlook, for example, into a riveting dissertation, which would have his audience leaning forward expectantly waiting for the next linguistic triple somersault and pike. Give him a written speech and he was often dreary.

Gough Whitlam, on the other hand, was brilliant delivering a formal, polished written speech. The language, ideas and delivery would thrill listeners. Let him speak without a script and he could bore for Australia. When he was in South Australia he would often turn to one of his great passions – the national railway system. Gough wanted to rid Australia of the dysfunctional separate state rail systems with their different gauges and when he was PM he offered to buy them from the states – only SA premier Don Dunstan accepted the offer. So in SA he liked to celebrate this great exemplar of commonwealth and state cooperation by Labor leaders acting in the national interest. All of his supporters in SA agreed with him, we just didn't need to hear about it every time he visited.

On one occasion at a Fabian Society launch, in a hotel dining room near Trades Hall on South Terrace, Gough as guest speaker spoke on his favourite topic for well over an hour; as we had all been drinking beforehand the stampede to the toilets after he'd finished was furious. On that same occasion I introduced myself to the great man; I was then the ALP organiser. Gough shook my hand and in his Gough voice said, 'Tell me, comrade, are you some kind of dago?' Given that an Italian taxi driver had asked me the same question that very day, albeit using less offensive language, I thought my looks must be revealing something unknown in my genes.

Bob Hawke was also a great public speaker and much better when giving a stump speech, especially when comparing the Opposition's position to his own. His lawyer's training was always on display on these occasions and he would ruthlessly examine, piece by piece, the arguments used by his opponents and destroy them by the force of his logic before putting the facts in support of his own position.

I was often described as passionate by people hearing my speeches – especially the ones given 'off the cuff' or from basic notes, rather than from polished prepared scripts. These informal speeches could be described as 'stump' speeches, so named because of the practice of politicians in 19th-century America campaigning from town to town using the same speech, while standing on a tree stump. In my case my stump speeches covered topics like saving the River Murray, the need for the New RAH, and dealing with the obesity epidemic. These were the speeches I gave frequently: on riverbanks, in hospital lecture theatres, Labor Party sub-branches, town halls; times when reading a speech would seem strange and artificial. Where it would look like I didn't know what I was talking about. These were speeches designed to persuade and they were packed with what I hoped were killer facts, which I could rattle off like a contestant in a quiz show. And I did feel passionate about these issues.

Many writers of books about selling say that good sales people are the ones who believe in the products they sell and don't sell the products they don't believe in. As I found out as a 16 year old working in a department store, selling came easily to me; if I liked something I could sell it.

In politics the truly successful ministers are the ones who fall in love with their portfolios, because they then become passionate about their responsibilities, making it easier for them to persuade others.

MEDIA

If everything is amplified, we hear nothing.
Jon Stewart (1962–), US political satirist

I remember clearly the first time I was on TV and the thrill it gave me.

At Christmas 1956, my mother, Moira, and sister Kathleen and I travelled to Sydney by train from Tamworth, where my father, Jack, ran the Ampol office. We were spending the school holidays with my grandparents who lived in the inner-western suburb of Ashfield. We arrived at their home late in the afternoon – my sister, then aged six, and I, aged seven, were very excited to see television for the first time.

TV had come to Sydney in September that year and my grandparents were early adopters. Kathleen and I were keen to watch *The Mickey Mouse Club*, but for some reason my grandmother insisted we watch *The Captain Fortune Show*, a homegrown kids' program – the likes of which can still be seen on TV. After a few minutes it became apparent why. This beautiful Irish woman had arranged for the good captain to welcome 'John and Kathy Hill down from Tamworth for their holidays'.

Shortly after the 1997 state election Gary Gray, who was then ALP national secretary and the person who coined the title 'Captain Wacky' for PM Paul Keating, arranged a media training course for a number of newly elected MPs, including me.

We flew into Melbourne for a couple of days for a series of lectures and practical workshops. The star presenter was Anthony Simcoe, who had played the part of Steve Kerrigan in that year's iconic Australian film *The Castle*; 'tell them they're dreaming', 'that one goes straight to the poolroom', and 'the whole vibe of the thing' have all become part of our popular idiom.

It was a useful experience – I learnt a lot about how to use voice and body language to get a point over; some of it pretty obvious, for example: don't point, it's too aggressive; use open hands palms up to be inclusive. The course involved mock interviews and a collective critique of each other's performance. Being able to communicate through the media is an essential skill for a minister and like anything else you can improve by going through a structured process of learning. Some people, of course, seem to be naturals; others seem only to get worse, no matter how much experience and training they receive.

In US politics the standout TV performers have to include Kennedy, Reagan, Clinton and Obama. George Bush was pretty bad at it, but it didn't stop his re-election. Nixon is an interesting case study – he famously is said to have won the 1960 presidential debate with Kennedy with the radio audience, but lost it on television. His perspiration made him look dodgy – which he certainly was. In 1952, Nixon was fighting to keep his place as vice-presidential candidate. His famous 'fireside' TV advertisement with Pat, his wife, and his dog Checkers, where he addressed accusations of corruption, was a masterpiece in manipulation – or 'spin' as we now describe it.

In Australia, Bob Hawke was superb as was, eventually and in a different way, John Howard. In both cases they, even when dissembling, seemed to be able to project their essential characters and appeal to Australians. Their qualities of determination, strength of character and leadership came through.

In 1996, in an extraordinary SA Liberal leadership coup – reminiscent of the later Gillard/Rudd battle – John Olsen replaced first-term premier, Dean Brown. Apparently, many of the first-term Liberal backbenchers who had won their seats on Brown's very long shirt tails became convinced that only Olsen would enable them to survive. It was not hard to understand why – Mike Rann, as Opposition leader may not have been popular but, like Tony Abbott, he was very successful at dominating the night's media with his strident criticisms of Brown and his government.

Brown had a slightly hesitant style and in parliament was easily overshadowed by John Olsen, who was a masterful and confident debater. So the backbenchers turned to Olsen. He had energy and policy focus but was woeful on television. It is hard to think of another leader who presented more poorly. His skill and authority just disappeared on TV. Like Nixon, his swarthy complexion didn't help – but his authority was undermined by the way his speaking manner, confident and dominating in parliament, became simpering and wishy-washy on TV. Maybe he had been to a media training course and been told to tone down his naturally aggressive style. I had some experience in this regard with Mike Rann.

As ALP secretary between 1994 and 1997 it was my job to brief the leader on research. And one of the research findings was that Mike was coming over pretty poorly on TV. Surprising, given his nickname 'Media Mike', based on his background as a journalist, and his outstanding ability to use the media to get stories into the public realm. The public, or at least the swinging voters we surveyed, didn't like his voice or the way he pushed towards the camera. They thought him too aggressive. Try telling that to a naturally aggressive person! Mike worked at it and toned down his approach considerably – and the focus groups complained he wasn't strong enough. My job was to pass on this information too. I thought Mike would burst a gasket when I delivered it.

Regardless of the advice from me, the focus groups, confidantes and complete strangers, Mike managed to hit the right note at the right time – the televised leaders' debate on the Tuesday before the 1997 election. He absolutely 'creamed' Olsen and a surge of support showed up in the polls. But I didn't need to see the polls – the next morning I felt it at on the verandahs of the homes I was doorknocking in Seaford Rise. I had spent hundreds of days over six years knocking on thousands and thousands of doors but I have never experienced a more positive response than I did that morning – people seemed to be jumping out of their skin to tell me they were voting for Mike and Labor and, of course, me.

Television is an amplifier – it adds kilos to your weight; if you are unshaven you look bearded, if you are tired you look exhausted (a comment commonly thrown at me), and if you are aggressive you look ferocious. What works in parliament or a hall or on the front steps of parliament doesn't work on TV. I recall John Hewson, the Liberal leader during the 'Fightback/True Believers' 1993 election, addressing rallies around Australia, trying to build up excitement for change. It probably felt great at the rally where a few thousand faithful and curious cheered the message; here he would have looked strong and charismatic. But on TV that night he came across as a scary and slightly unhinged bloke – definitely not prime ministerial.

Paul Keating, our most interesting prime minister ever and certainly one of the most charming at a personal level, completely dominated political debate for years. But he was undone by John

Howard, who came across as a humble, awkward suburban lawyer with the good sense to be polite and mild mannered when he visited our lounge rooms.

At the media training seminar arranged by Gary Gray, one of the key messages was not to worry about the question asked by the journalist but to give the answer you want. Stick to your message! Message discipline is considered extremely important, especially in election campaigns. Vickie Chapman and Steven Griffiths, Liberal frontbenchers during the 2010 state election, seriously veered from the Liberal message in the key days before polling day with serious consequences for their side. Some claim it was enough to get Labor over the line.

Greg Kelton on 27 March in his post-election wrap wrote:

> *One week before last Saturday's election, Labor was – in the words of a very senior Party source – 'gone for all money' …. Three days later … Vickie Chapman came to the rescue and a few days after that comments from … Stephen Griffiths about hospital costings being 'spin' further boosted Labor's stocks … it was Chapman's refusal to rule out a challenge to Opposition Leader Isobel Redmond which gave Labor the most heart.*

A media conference should work along these lines:

Minister: *'Thanks for coming today to the launch of "An apple a day keeps the doctor away". The Government will make sure that every school child in SA eats their daily apple. This will be good for kids, take pressure off our busy doctors, and boost the income of our struggling apple producers. Any questions?'*

Journalist: *'Minister, what do you say to claims that thousands of patients are waiting too long for surgery?'*

Minister: *'This Government will make sure that an apple every day will keep doctors away from our children and allow them to concentrate on the truly sick.'*

Journalist: 'The AMA says that 10,000 patients each year are denied life-saving surgery because of a lack of hospital beds.'

Minister: 'Every apple that keeps the doctor away is an investment in the future health of our citizens ...'

And so it goes on; the aim is to only say what you want to say, so that media coverage is about your story. But it doesn't really work that way. These interviews can go on for quite some time until one side or other gives up. And often it is the politician who walks away, which the media love of course, and the TV image that night demonstrates the truism that a picture is worth a thousand words.

A couple of days after my retirement announcement in January 2013, at my last 'presser' on a blazing hot day outside the Lyell McEwin Hospital to announce the decision not to proceed with upgrading some wards, I held my ground. With reporters and advisors practically passing out with heat stroke I relentlessly answered every facile and repetitive question about whether or not I had been sacked: Why wasn't I wearing a tie? (It was hot!) Would I keep my car and driver? (No.) It became a battle of wills and stamina, especially with Tom Richardson, Channel 9's then senior reporter who led the questioning. I was determined there would be no final shot of me 'walking' and eventually the reporters gave up.

Early on in my career I decided to ignore the advice that I should only give the rehearsed grab – with some exceptions. When environment minister I was asked about plans by the Howard Government to build a radioactive waste dump in the Woomera Prohibited Area, where there were still ambitions to launch rockets. My grab, totally rehearsed, was, 'You don't need to be a rocket scientist to know that building a radioactive waste dump at Woomera is a bad idea.'

Generally, I found I performed better at media interviews if I attempted to give a real and truthful answer to the questions asked, rather than the rehearsed line. I also found I enjoyed the interviews more and, importantly, received the respect of the journalists who knew I didn't dissemble. That translated through the cameras and tubes into the lounge rooms. The feedback I received about my news grabs was that I generally looked tired but came over as honest and straightforward.

I don't want to suggest I was recklessly outspoken like the character Warren Beatty played in the 1998 film *Bulworth*. You may recall that Bulworth, a cynical political figure, decides to tell it exactly how it is following a series of misadventures, until he is assassinated by vested interests.

I do know my approach was not the one preferred by the premier's office. My first media advisor Nick Talbot used to plead with me to adopt a sharper political line in interviews, following a 'bottralling' by Jill Bottrall, who was then Mike Rann's chief media advisor. Jill is the only person I know who contributed a word to the language: to be 'bottralled' is like being bollocked, but harder and sharper. Jill used to apply her skills to journalists, staffers and sometimes ministers without fear or favour. I liked Jill – she was only doing her job, which usually was to pass on a message from the premier.

At the time we had been running a campaign against the Howard Government, which wanted to build a radioactive waste dump in South Australia to store Australia's radioactive waste. The issue was one of some urgency as the Commonwealth wanted to rebuild the Lucas Heights nuclear facility. In order to appease that local community they wanted to shift the waste stored there to a permanent facility and they identified sites in outback SA as suitable. Their only problem was that South Australians were overwhelmingly opposed, so it was a good political issue for us – especially as the state Liberals were in favour of their Federal colleagues' proposition. We were the ones standing up for SA.

My argument was that if it's safe enough to have a reactor in Sydney then it should be safe enough to have its waste stored there as well. The Feds were really dealing with the politics of NSW – we the politics of SA.

There was plenty of media interest and Mike Rann ran a very strong and ultimately successful campaign – even, against expectations, gaining a Federal Court victory. During the debate many questions were raised about the radioactive waste stored at various sites in SA, including the Royal Adelaide Hospital. The Opposition put the proposition that South Australians would be better off if our own waste was removed from current locations and stored in a permanent waste facility funded and managed by the Feds. Given the uncertainty of the outcome of our campaign, I was keen to leave the door open and in response to questions about whether we would use the Commonwealth facility, if it were opened, I said that we probably would. This approach didn't go down well with the premier's office – we were running a black and white campaign and I was introducing grey.

There is no doubt that Mike Rann's approach was successful. Whatever the issue, the media and voters had no doubt as to his position. Mike used to say he liked to boil issues down to a headline – his experience as a journalist showing through. This approach paid huge dividends for Labor with issues like the nuclear waste dumps.

Another key issue was what was known as the Nemer case. Nemer was a young man who escaped a custodial sentence for shooting an innocent man in his eye, following recommendations from our Director of Public Prosecutions. The community was outraged by the lenient sentence. Nemer became the symbol of Labor's tough law and order stance when following the government's insistence, the DPP lodged an appeal against the sentence that saw Nemer serve gaol time.

Mike's green credentials were highlighted by his 'obsession' with wind power and the fact our state had over half Australia's wind turbines. His economic development credentials were promoted through his support for the Olympic Dam mine expansion and plans to build warships at Port Adelaide.

'No dumps', 'Nemer', 'wind power', 'Olympic Dam', and 'warships' cut through at the 2006 election. We 'smashed' the Opposition with the slogan 'Rann Gets Results'.

Greg Mackie, then executive director of Arts SA, gave me a very useful book: *Don't Think of an Elephant* by George Lakoff – a deep analysis of the use of language in American politics and particularly the use of certain phrases by the Republicans to demonise their opponents. For example Democrats are regularly described by Republicans as 'big taxing, big spending', while Republicans describe themselves as being in favour of 'low taxes and small government'. Those labels resonate with voters. However, if the Republicans were to say that they intended to cut spending on important programs in health and education to fund tax cuts for their wealthy supporters it wouldn't go down so well.

Lakoff's title is the key to understanding his thesis. If you say to someone 'don't think of an elephant', then the first thing they think of is an elephant. You cannot help it.

In my first interview as health minister, on the well-manicured lawns in front of Government House, I was mindful of this advice. The interview went along these lines:

Journalist: 'How does it feel being given the poisoned chalice portfolio?'

Me: 'I am honoured to be health minister – the provision of a good health service is at the heart of what a Labor government is about.'

J: 'You've just been given the worst job in politics, how can you say that?'

Me: 'The worst job in politics is being leader of the Opposition. Just ask Rob Kerin' (then Opposition leader and under enormous pressure to perform or leave).

J: 'You have a health system in crisis, what are you going to do to fix it?'

Me: 'We have a very good health system in SA – my job is to make it an excellent one.'

The trick is to answer the question directly without using the negative language and assumptions of the questioner. In seven years as health minister only once that I am aware of did I use the word 'crisis' in an interview. To journalists everything that happens is a 'crisis', 'scandal' or 'blow-out'. I cringe when I see ministers in interviews using the language of the media to explain the situations they face. The phrase 'there is no crisis', using Lakoff's thesis, screams 'crisis' as loudly as if the minister had agreed 'there is a crisis'. Even worse, not only is there a crisis but a minister in denial.

Very rarely in public life are there real crises. An out-of-control bushfire or flood – yes; and usually only for a day or two. Governments and communities face problems every day, which they deal with appropriately every day. The media report conflicts and problems – and the more hyped the better. In doing that they are pandering to their audience, which might deny it likes the violence and conflict – but let's face it, they do, that's why they watch night after night. Peering at the big bad world from the snugness of the hearth.

Oppositions play the same role – overegging whatever happens and inflating it into a 'crisis' or 'disaster' and calling for a Royal Commission or a ministerial resignation or some such.

My theory is that the smaller the community, the more the minor issues are magnified into 'disasters'. People like to read and watch stories about their own community; there is very little interest in international events, unless they involve Australians or international celebrities or truly fully fledged disasters, like a tsunami. Our TV news services have as many minutes as a news service in New York or London and our newspapers as many pages so the most newsworthy issue in our community on a particular day gets the same level of coverage as the biggest issues in those larger cities.

As a consequence of this catastrophising our community is overly worried about its personal safety, financial security, future prospects, key institutions, public morality and political integrity. Rather than celebrating the fact we truly live in 'paradise' – as Nobel Laureate and immigrant to South Australia, J.M. Coetzee, describes this place – we worry about everything. It's described as the Adelaide disease by some – that sense of defeat that pervades any change, and which is accompanied, contradictorily, by a desire for change. As someone put it recently: We want progress, but we hate change.

This is not a new phenomenon, as George Reid our fourth prime minister noted in his autobiography *My Reminiscences* published in 1917: 'Kingston, the Premier of South Australia, could hold his own in any intellectual or political struggle. In a larger sphere than the South Australian he would have been a much greater man. As communities diminish in size, personal antagonisms seem to increase in size. Mr Kingston ... seemed to arouse ridiculous hatred amongst his political opponents.'

I don't blame the media for this. Individual media networks are like political parties, they do their market research and compete for market share, they win or lose ratings rounds.

One thing I do criticise the media for is the kind of reporting that purports to provide balance in the presentation of news, but in facts distorts the news by giving equal weight to all opinions, without rigorous investigation – a false or exaggerated claim can be made and reported; the 'correction' will come later if you're lucky.

One very nasty example of this was when the doctors' union (SASMOA) made the sensational claim to the media, not to me as the responsible minister, that the Lyell McEwin Hospital emergency department was so busy that doctors were forced to treat patients on the floor. Their president claimed that while he hadn't seen it himself it had been reported to him. He also claimed that the ED had run out of oxygen. As Ruth Awbery, my media advisor, pointed out, these claims were so sensational they would take root quickly through continual retelling in media reports; I needed to act swiftly to knock them on the head.

I asked the health CE David Swan to arrange for an investigation of the claims and he commissioned Dr Stephen Christley, Chief Public Health Officer for SA Health, originally from NSW and an experienced clinician. He acted quickly, visited the hospital, spoke with staff, checked records and found no evidence whatsoever to the claims.

Christley found that the day in question 'was a very busy day' but 'no patients were treated on the floor'. He found that the story appears to have developed after a comment from a busy nurse to a doctor looking for a bed on which to treat a patient that 'if they needed to do something urgently they would need to treat them on the floor'. Someone else relayed that and through a 'Chinese whispers effect' Dr Pope made his claim – which was then repeated starkly throughout the media. No objectivity, no seeking of evidence – just a sensational claim made by a doctor, which must therefore be true. The correction, when it came, received some coverage but nowhere near the amount received by the original claim.

On 23 May 2012, ABC News posted the story that SA Health would investigate the Salaried Medical Officers Association's claims: 'The association says patients were forced to lie on the floor last week ... when the hospital's emergency department ran out of spare beds and trolleys.' The ABC quoted Dr Pope (the president) calling for the report to be made public.

On 15 June 2012, the ABC News reported there was no evidence patients were treated on the floor, nor that the ED had run out of oxygen.

In response Andrew Murray, SASMOA's paid official, was reported as saying the association 'never claimed patients were treated on the floor, only that doctors were asked to do so'.

During the annual estimates hearings on 20 June 2012, the then shadow Minister for Health, Martin Hamilton-Smith (one of six I faced as health minister), asked me a series of questions about the episode, taking as his starting point the revised position of the Association put by Murray on 15 June.

Fortunately, I was able to rely on another ABC report – this time from Matt and Dave's ABC morning program of 23 May, where Dr Pope, SASMOA president, was interviewed. Matt Abraham's and David Bevan's program on the ABC's local radio network station 891 is an Adelaide institution; a unique combination of politics, news, music and suburban life, with plenty of humour laced with sarcasm.

David Bevan asked Dr Pope:

Can you confirm you don't have any doubts that this incident did occur ... a patient or patients plural were forced to lie on the floor at the Lyell McEwin in the last week or so and that's where they were being treated?

Dr Pope responded:

That's right. What happened was that the hospital and the emergency department ran out of beds and barouches. There were patients who needed to lie down to be assessed for their conditions and there was no option but for the people to use the floor. So medical staffs were seriously asked if they would see and examine and treat people on the floor ... nobody was on the floor for any length of time but that was the situation faced by medical staff at the time.

Mr Hamilton-Smith's comment on hearing this extract was to say to the committee:

We will not waste any more time of estimates on this point, but my view is that you have used a bit of licence as well in interpreting Dr Pope's remarks.

I leave it to the reader to assess who was exercising licence here.

No retraction, correction or apology came from the association, Dr Pope or Mr Murray; but thank god for Matt and Dave! The only media outlet I am aware of to closely question the claims. Once again the reputation of our excellent healthcare system and one of our hospitals in particular had been besmirched by an inaccurate claim, untested by the media, and which may have lead to patients making poor decisions because they were fearful of the treatment they might receive at Lyell Mc.

My first Matt and Dave interview, as a minister, happened on my second day in the job. They asked me why I hadn't fixed some problem or other in the environment area. I think my response was along the lines of 'Give us a break; I haven't been in the job 24 hours yet!' I don't think either they or their listeners ever care what the minister's reason is – there's a problem and it's your job to fix it, no excuses! Fair enough.

In almost 11 years as a minister rarely a week went by that I wasn't cross-examined, poked, accused, joked with or challenged on their morning program. Many weeks I was the minister *du jour* two or three times – depending on the issue. The environment and health portfolios always had something of interest happening. That means that I did in the order of 500 or so live interviews with two of the best informed, most intelligent and, at times, most offensive interviewers in the business.

Matt's and Dave's specialty is what I call the 'twist and turn'. They like to take something you say and then use it against you (the twist) or jump from one issue to another (the turn). The fact there are two of them against one of you makes these interviews a challenging experience. I can't say I ever looked forward to these interviews, but I usually felt OK once they were over. To be honest, I generally enjoyed the contest – a seasoned gladiator in the arena with two growling middle-aged lions. What I enjoyed most was going into the ABC studio at Collinswood for an extended interview with phone-in discussions with the public. Generally, these interviews were longer, more relaxed, and with fewer traps.

One of my most unpleasant radio interviews was on 18 November 2010, following the announcement that Tony Sherbon was resigning as Health CE to take up a national job. His wife Catherine Hockley, my then chief of staff, was leaving too. I agreed to go on the Matt and Dave show on morning radio to talk about it. On this occasion, the mangled language shows

MEDIA

how tense it became. Matt Abraham asked me about Tony's and Catherine's relationship:

> Abraham: *Is that a bit of a cosy arrangement ...?*
>
> Me: *Oh come on ... I'm not sure what you're suggesting there, Matthew*
>
> A: *Well, I'm just wondering whether you lose a lack (sic) of distance, I suppose between your ... You'd have to say it's quite an extraordinary chain of command, having the Health Minister and his Chief of Staff and his CEO ...*
>
> M: *Well, it just so happens that ... my Chief of Staff was in working for me and she met the CEO after he was appointed ... it wasn't as if it was the other direction ... it's been managed very well and I think it's appalling that you would suggest there's anything improper about it*
>
> A: *I'm not suggesting anything improper, Minister*
>
> M: *Well, what are you suggesting ... what do you mean by 'cosy' then?*
>
> A: *Well in terms of ... I'm asking you whether you feel you would ... in having that close relationship, which I think you'd have to say is unique in the state Government ... whether there is a lack of impartiality? I don't know*
>
> M: *Well, of course there is (sic) but you are suggesting something improper by asking that question, there is absolutely nothing improper about the way both of them have carried out their jobs ...*

Over the years I was astonished by the number of people, both strangers and acquaintances, who would comment that they liked hearing me on Matt's and Dave's show and who would compliment me on my performance. What people seemed to like was that I generally appeared calm, that I was straight with my answers, and that I stood up to their occasional 'bullying'. On the whole I think it was worthwhile appearing. I nearly always agreed to go on, which they seemed to respect, and they often let their listeners know how available I was. At times I felt like the go-to or default minister because others made themselves unavailable or simply refused to go on.

Some would argue that there is often little point going on these kinds of shows – relatively few people listen and the audience is generally older with established political points of view. Why go on and potentially make the issue worse? There is obviously merit in this argument; from a strict media management point of view it makes sense. And maybe my point of view is old-fashioned, but I think that if you can't stand up to tough media interviews you really shouldn't be in the job. It's like wanting to be a top cricketer without facing fast bowling. Ministers should front for a variety of reasons: it's part of their job, it toughens them (or destroys them) and helps build their reputation for openness (the public hates politicians who hide behind media management).

There was one extended period when Mike Rann, not because of any lack of toughness, refused to appear on the show and there was some pressure on other ministers to follow suit. Most complied with alacrity, but I and a few others ignored the 'ban'.

Interviews with Matt's and David's competitor Leon Byner on 5AA are a different experience altogether and harder to predict. Byner, who I first heard on radio in the mid '70s when he was a pop station DJ, had morphed over time into a 'shock jock', in the style of 2GB's Alan Jones. The role of the 'shock jock' is to express strong, often extreme, points of view and then get stuck into the politician willing to put a different point of view.

With Matt and Dave I knew that various points of view would be put to me and pursued; if I could mount a good argument they would accept the logic and move on. This rarely happened with Leon. Leon would usually start an interview with an 'editorial' that relied heavily on information provided by one of his contacts or experts (often someone at odds with the government's position) and then the interview would begin. I think it is fair to say I rarely if ever convinced Leon his original position or his experts were wrong; once he had found his spot, there he would stay. Appearing on his program was frustrating and usually futile. The other problem was that he would never accept anyone other than the minister. Depending on the issue, it was often more sensible to put up the public servant who knew about the details of something, especially if it were a technical matter. Most media understood this – but not Leon. But if I knew the issue, no matter how technical, had become political and an Opposition spokesperson was on, I would appear too.

An indiscreet or ill-thought-out comment on morning radio could lead to a day of media. So an appearance on a program with a small audience could generate the 'story of the day' – which would then be followed up by the really big audience programs: the evening news services. Usually, not a story to the government's liking.

But generally, even with falling readership and on-line competition, the *Advertiser* more often than not is responsible for the story of the day. Driven in part by its need to generate sales through attention-capturing 'splashes' but also the 'leaks' and 'drops' provided to it by political parties and other organisations.

There are many in the Labor Party who regard the *Advertiser* as not much more than a Liberal Party publication. There are good reasons for this view, not least of which is the general News Ltd support for conservative political parties in America, Britain and Australia. The almost continual campaigning of the Australian newspaper against the former federal Labor Government is a case in point. It's true the *Advertiser* often criticises the government – sometimes unfairly, in my view – and can be very pro-business in its attitudes, but I don't see it as anti-Labor or even pro-Liberal. In fact, the *Advertiser* has on more occasions than most in the past 20 years advocated a vote for Labor at state election time.

Under its long-serving boss Mel Mansell, the paper has taken a positive approach to many government initiatives – in particular, the New RAH development. This was in keeping with the paper's ethos to promote positive stories about South Australia, an important approach given the tendency to gloom and despair so easily exhibited by South Australians.

I like Mel and enjoy his company and Ruth Awbery (and before her, Catherine Hockley) and I would have an annual lunch with Mel and one of his senior reporters, usually the then health reporter Tory Shepherd. These were fun affairs: Mel and Tory are good company. On one memorable occasion lunch spread into dinner. We were in the clubby Chesser Cellars, presided over by Primo Caon who had much earlier run Charlie Brown's Bistro with his brother Giocondo ... where famously Don Dunstan's lover and staffer, John Ceruto, had been 'given' work experience. (On another occasion, after reading Des Ryan's *It's Grossly Improper* about the Dunstan downfall, I arranged a lunch at Chesser Cellars with Des and John Bannon to learn more about those days.)

No matter how long the lunches went and how many bottles of wine were drunk these events never got out of control. Mel always called me 'Minister' and while we talked about issues of the day no state secrets were given up. I imagine many people reading this might conclude that these were just drunken indulgences enjoyed by a couple of powerful blokes – and in part that's true. But these lunches helped build a relationship – not an improper one, but one useful to both sides. Mel and I enjoyed friendly relations and, importantly, trusted each other.

Some politicians go out of their way to court journalists and confide in them about colleagues and policy initiatives. Some leak against their own side. Until 2010 I don't think there had been a single leak out of the Rann Cabinet. Following the reshuffle, leaking began. Those of us who had been around for a while had our suspicions about who the culprit was. But, of course, it's very hard to prove. This particular person, who was not popular with colleagues, always seemed to get an easy ride in the media.

While I enjoyed my annual lunch with Mel and Tory, most of my dealings with journalists were on the other side of the microphone or in informal situations such as waiting for the interview to begin or travelling together to a remote location.

Mostly reporters are affable and you can, in these informal situations, believe you share a friendship. This is a mistake – no matter how chummy they are, given an opportunity they will slit your throat and use against you whatever they have gleaned during one of these chats.

Mike Smithson, the senior reporter for Channel 7, was always 'hail fellow well met', but wouldn't hesitate to put the boot in – which he did to me on several occasions, but at least his criticisms were balanced with the occasional word of praise when he thought I deserved it.

His competitor, Channel 9's Tom Richardson, was not nearly as charming; in fact he always seemed dyspeptic – and he too could put the boot in, on one occasion making fun of me for having a coughing fit while launching a new health service (admittedly not a good look). At least he didn't pretend to be nice.

One genuinely nice person was the late Greg Kelton, a senior political reporter for the *Advertiser* since the 1970s until his retirement in 2012. Greg had seen and heard it all and knew everyone in town. But he had also learned how to have an easy life – he liked to leave the office at five to catch his bus home so he preferred his copy in early. This approach doesn't leave much room for analysis or balance. It's not that Greg was particularly pro-Opposition or pro-government – whoever got to him first was likely to dominate the story. The alternative point of view would come in the last sentence or, if significant enough, the next day. I always thought that once Greg made up his mind about an issue he would repeat it *ad nauseum*.

Greg developed a theory that as health minister I was 'Mr Teflon' and I kept health off the front pages. This was flattering, but untrue. Health was regularly on the front pages for one reason or another. However, I managed generally to deal with the issues, whatever they were, without causing too much damage to myself or the government – hence the 'Teflon' tag.

By the beginning of the second quarter of 2012, Greg decided I was no longer 'Mr Teflon' and, in a series of articles, stated I was 'under pressure'; these stories were often accompanied by a very unflattering photograph that made me look both worried and old.

The interview that gave rise to that claim and the photograph happened outside the SA Health building on Hindmarsh Square one afternoon in April, following a poor auditor-general's report and, in particular, a claim that the department was running two sets of books relating to overseas travel by public servants. Martin Hamilton-Smith jumped on to the issue. He was my shadow – but in reality it was Opposition leader Isobel Redmond's job he was after; consequently, everything he said or did at that time was given much greater attention than was usual for a shadow minister.

I turned up to the interview confident about the issues. The reality was that the Auditor-General's Department had got it wrong – there weren't two sets of books; there was a register for information that was eventually transferred to the formal document. It had always been done that way and never previously commented on by the AG. The other AG issues, which were real and serious, were being properly addressed. Like all the other front-page stories I had confronted, I was well briefed by my staff, confident about the solutions, and ready to explain it all to the media and public. Leah Manuel, the staffer who accompanied me to the interview, commented on how relaxed I had been in the interview. She stated I was 'under no pressure' whatsoever.

Kelton's article and photograph the next day told a different story. The photograph used was taken when I made a characteristic gesture of scratching my forehead; that gesture, my open mouth (probably talking), and the lighting emphasising lined skin all contributed to make me look old, worried and confused – in other words, under pressure!

In the final paragraph of Kelton's story my response to the question about 'pressure' is quoted: 'I have now faced five Opposition spokespeople on health and they have all made exaggerated claims which have distorted the facts and tried to make things look worse than they really are. I am absolutely used to it. I know the health system we have is far better than the one we inherited 10 years ago.'

It is the job of shadow ministers to hold ministers to account. The six I fronted used the same strategy – everything that happened pointed to a 'crisis' in health, which was run by a hopeless minister. I was described by Hamilton-Smith as 'Crazy John' (which offended the mental health community), for being 'tired' and (implied) 'old'. Others called me 'arrogant' and a 'bully', and Vickie Chapman bizarrely had a go at me on one occasion for being a former teacher (what could I possibly know about health?) and from New South Wales (what did I know about SA?).

ON BEING A MINISTER

Years before, I attended the funeral of Des Corcoran, a former premier and old-style Labor leader. I had known Des, although not well, and went to his funeral out of respect for him, his family and his position in the Labor movement. The next day the *Advertiser* ran a photograph of me outside the church, wiping tears from my eyes, suggesting these were tears of grief. Anyone who knows me knows that I suffer from a chronic condition that causes my eyes to water, more or less continuously – especially in bright light. I wondered what members of Des's family must have thought.

On another occasion, at a hastily called press conference on a Friday evening to report the first death in Australia from the swine flu epidemic then panicking the world, the *Advertiser* photographer took a photo of me leaning against a wall, eyes downcast, while the chief medical officer spoke to reporters. Its publication the next day, with an appropriate caption, made me look caring and concerned. Both true enough – but at the time the photo was taken, my mind was miles away.

One of the earliest press photographs of me that I can recall was taken in 1982, when I was the Labor candidate in the Mitcham by-election, brought about by the appointment by Liberal premier David Tonkin of sitting Democrat MP Robin Millhouse to the Supreme Court. This was an ill-fated attempt by Tonkin, another genuinely nice man, to gain an extra seat before the next election. The Democrats were keen to retain the seat and endorsed yet another nice person, Heather Southcott; Robert Worth (whose wife, Trish, eventually became Federal MP for Adelaide) was the Liberal. Labor had no hope of winning – our vote was about 25 per cent – but we could help Heather by running third. This was a difficult strategy for me because I wanted to impress with a big swing to show my 'outstanding' campaigning skills to a Party that didn't know me then, but would have seen me (accurately enough) as a scruffy, university-educated yuppie. My campaign slogan was: Mitcham an up-Hill Battle. It kind of satisfied both the Party's need for me to come third, and my own ego. We had fun on the campaign and it certainly gave me experience, exposure and connections.

A week before election day, Matthew Abraham, at that time a political reporter for the *Advertiser*, came to my house with photographer Tony Lewis. I can't remember much about the interview, but I do remember the published photograph and its caption. In the garden of the Unley Park former boarding house that ten of us had bought, there was a non-functioning, coin-operated horse – the sort found in every shopping centre and used to reward kids. Why we had it I don't know. Matthew persuaded me to sit on the horse for the photographer. Next day it was published with the caption: 'Labor candidate flogging a dead horse'.

My view about media management is straightforward: be available, be honest, be yourself. You can't worry about the day-to-day reporting – you can only hope that over time people will get to see enough of you to make a fair judgement. If you don't like the way you are reported don't watch. The longer I served as a minister the less and less I watched TV news or listened to radio. I had staff and a very vigilant wife who would tell me what was going on – and of course I had media monitoring. I found it less stressful that way. I know some politicians obsess about media treatment and compulsively watch and read everything presented about themselves. Therein madness lies.

Errors of fact occur all the time in media reports; either they are minor or so obviously wrong they are not worth worrying about. However, if I thought the media had got it really wrong I'd write a letter to the editor to at least correct the record (important historically, I think) or, in the case of the electronic record, my media advisor would call to put my point of view. Sometimes it worked, and a follow up would appear, but TV in particular is so ephemeral that the circus had usually moved on.

Mostly, I would just cop whatever was said and move on too – 'there is always another day' is my attitude. However, the exception was when I believed I had been defamed. The fact that this occurred only rarely speaks well of our media. The first case involved *Today Tonight*.

A few years ago my son Eric, a lawyer, contacted me to let me know that Channel 7, in his view, had repeatedly defamed me in a promotion about my failure, and my department's, to pay an employee. The promotion, which featured me prominently in an unflattering way, was for a piece going to air the following Monday on the *Today Tonight* program. The promotion was repeated numerous times over the weekend. Concerned about the allegations, I sought advice.

The allegation turned out to be a complete invention by the alleged victim, who had some sort of grievance based on an unrealistic expectation. One of my staff members rang the person who claimed to have documents proving her claim; the staffer travelled to her home in the outer suburbs to be told that the documents were in fact in Port Pirie. The long and the short of it was the woman had not worked for the department for over a year, her work had been temporary in nature, and she had been properly remunerated. All of this was established on the Monday by my staff and departmental officers.

If the allegations had been put to me by *Today Tonight* all of this would have been revealed. Unfortunately, the program, for whatever reason, chose to go with an unsubstantiated and damaging claim against me and my 'uncaring' bureaucracy. One of Mike Rann's favourite statements, used frequently and ironically, applied on this occasion: 'Don't worry about the quality – just feel the width.' Armed with the facts I rang the head of Channel 7 in Adelaide, Tony Davidson, a decent and community-minded person, told him the facts, said I didn't want to pursue legal redress, but wanted a retraction and apology. To his credit, he rapidly agreed and we nutted out a form of words, which were read by the presenter at the head of the program and again the next day by Leon Byner on his 5AA program where the claims had also been made.

As satisfying as the apologies and retractions were, their formalistic and brief airings didn't really balance the repeated and inflammatory claims made. But still it was an apology and they can be hard to get. I knew, however, that revenge would be forthcoming and sure enough a week or so later the program found some other issue on which to attack me. That's political life – you have to absorb that; if you worry about every slight you go crazy.

The second case involved the late Christopher Pearson, a columnist for the *Australian* newspaper. I had known Pearson for years, from his time as editor and publisher of the *Adelaide Review*. I'd first met him when he seemed to be a Labor supporter – he had certainly attended a fundraising event for my Mitcham campaign in the early '80s – and I was well disposed towards him. The last time I can recall us meeting was when he argued for government assistance for the then struggling *Review*.

Eventually, he left the *Review* and worked for a time as a speechwriter for John Howard and then as a columnist for the *Australian*. In his 24–25 November 2012 column he attacked my advanced care directives legislation, which had passed through the House of Assembly and had yet to be considered by the Legislative Council. The legislation, which had been worked on for years, was intended to simplify the existing provisions without substantially changing their scope. We wanted to make it easier for people to let others know their wishes when certain health issues occurred, and create mechanisms so that those wishes could be implemented. Good modern policy supported by even the most religious members of the Labor Party right as well as most Liberals. This was not euthanasia and did not facilitate euthanasia.

Pearson's column didn't see it that way – he made the slippery slope argument; i.e. the legislation would lead to euthanasia, wrong but 'fair comment'. He also described me as a 'passionate' advocate for euthanasia; also wrong.

My principal objection was to the first lines of his column where he claimed I was introducing the new law in order to deal with budget pressures. To quote Pearson:

> South Australia under the Labor Government has regularly overspent the health budget by hundreds of millions of dollars in recent years.
>
> Former premier Mike Rann lacked the resolve to reduce the number of hospitals in metropolitan Adelaide, his power base, and its citizens are over-serviced.
>
> Health Minister John Hill has introduced a bill covering advanced-care directives, which will begin to address the issue by opening the way for practices currently categorised as euthanasia. We South Australians seldom do things by halves.

This deeply offended me and I believe damaged my reputation and imputed bad motives on my part. I wrote a letter to the editor seeking an apology. My media advisor Ruth Awbery followed this up with a discussion with the editor of the section in which the column appeared. Amazingly enough, the editor admitted

MEDIA

he hadn't read the column, but would ask Pearson to consider my request. Pearson refused – his claim, published as part of his eventual apology, was that the comment was 'intended as satire, in the tradition of Jonathan Swift's *Modest Proposal*, where he argues for converting Irish children surplus to the needs of the economy into food'. If so it was the only part of the column that was satire; the rest of it was an attack on the legislation – with no attempt, as is the right of a columnist, at balance. Certainly my views were not sought. The editor offered me space to express my opinion on the same page in a future edition. I rejected this option as to do so would acknowledge the right of Pearson to make his unfounded claims.

I now brought in the 'heavy guns', once again revealing the wisdom of having a lawyer as part of my team. I asked Anita Ewing, one of my ministerial advisors and a lawyer, to craft a tough letter. She did a spectacular job and shortly afterwards the *Australian* published an apology. That's all I wanted. I had no interest in pursuing a lengthy and possibly expensive legal case, though a number of colleagues have substantially bigger houses as a result of their successful defamation cases against various media outlets.

§

In the lead-up to the 2010 election, John McTernan, one of our splendid thinkers in residence addressed Cabinet about a range of issues associated with his residency. He had been focused on improving government service delivery through, as he described it, 'co-production'; in other words the involvement by the governed in the design of services provided to and for them. John had been a senior political advisor to British Labour prime ministers Blair and Brown and went on to become Julia Gillard's communications director.

Advancing communication between the governed and the governing was at the heart of John's thinking – and naturally, he was interested in social media. I think it is fair to say that most of us had heard of Facebook at that stage, but few if any had used social media. This discussion inspired the premier, Mike Rann, to open a Twitter account. The rest of us were pretty dubious and made the usual jokes about twits and so on. Now it's hard to imagine a serious political figure anywhere in the world who is not on Twitter; the US president, the Pope, Tony Abbott and Jay Weatherill are all part of the 'twittersphere'.

I resisted for several years until mid 2011, when with the encouragement of my staff, I signed up. It has been a revelation. It is now my principle source of breaking news – by 'following' many news outlets and individual journalists I know what is happening, virtually as it happens – ironically, meaning I no longer need to read, watch or listen to the outlets themselves. I have also been able to construct a diversity of sources that would be impossible to get in the mainstream media in Adelaide. It's a design-your-own news service, which puts enormous control in the consumer's hands. And what's even better, any consumer can contribute on an equal footing – the same 140-character restriction applies to everyone. You can challenge the source, criticise and praise it – all instantly.

For a politician it has a number of particular advantages. I know all the journalists 'followed' me when I was minister, as I 'followed' them. That meant that when an issue arose, say an allegation from an Opposition spokesperson or some other critic of government, I could get my response out quickly – to either correct the record or at least put my side. On one notable occasion my staff and I were able to turn around a press conference stunt by then health Opposition spokesman Stephen Marshall using quick staff work and Twitter.

Leah Manuel, a former media advisor to Jane Lomax-Smith during her time as education minister, joined me from Mike Rann's office after he stood down as premier. Leah had a fantastic no-nonsense approach to the world and joined my office as an advisor, particularly looking after my parliamentary briefs and keeping my fact file up to date.

It is especially important in a portfolio like health to have the latest facts at your fingertips. Someone is always going to the media making claims – an up-to-date fact can often kill off a story before it builds momentum. In her final throw of the dice, former Opposition leader Isobel Redmond replaced Martin Hamilton-Smith as her health shadow (after his failed leadership coup) with her new deputy, Steven Marshall. One quiet Sunday, the day before New Year's Eve 2012, Marshall called a press conference outside the Glenside Hospital and made the claim that the government had no current mental health strategy. He claimed our plan for 2007 to 2012 was about to run out.

Not a bad story for a new shadow on a quiet day and bound to get a good run. However, he was wrong and Leah found the evidence to prove it. On a Sunday, when practically everyone who could have helped was on leave or unavailable, she found our latest plan: 'Mental Health and Wellbeing Policy 2010–2015'. I was able to upload a copy of the front page of the new policy on to Twitter and issue a statement about Marshall's mistake – before his interview. Ruth got on to the media to make sure they knew of his error. His press conference was a train wreck – his lack of experience and preparation on show for all to see. He looked awkward and foolish. Great staff work.

As minister you are also 'followed' by people who work in

your agency, are advocates for it or users of it, and who like to hear about what's happening and will sometimes want specific information about changes. This direct connection via Twitter is unusual and powerful. Generally, phone calls, letters, emails, and visitors are controlled and managed without the minister directly getting involved. With Twitter it is direct and immediate. It's a good way to keep in touch – like shopping, catching a bus, or going to the footy.

It is also a way to show your humanity – to tweet about what rocks your boat in a personal way. I leavened my political tweets with descriptions and photos of local beaches and parks where Andrea and I walked, and photos and boasts about my fruit trees. In my last interview with Matt and Dave, Matt referred to my peaches and then segued into a comment about the health budget being pear-shaped. At least this showed he was following what I was saying.

Unfortunately, showing his humanity got one of my colleagues, the enthusiastic and honest Tom Kenyon, into trouble. He had tweeted about a birthday party where the partygoers were 'racing' sleepy lizards. The response resulted in him dropping out of Twitter for a while.

The strength can also be a weakness. The democracy of Twitter is wonderful; but it means the most awful, vicious and prejudiced individuals have access and can broadcast their vileness to whoever will listen. It also means they can abuse you as minister directly, and in the most horrible way. Fortunately, Twitter allows you to 'block' such nuisances; something I did rarely and only when the 'follower' became abusive.

7
CHALLENGES

We must accept life for what it actually is – a challenge to our quality without which we should never know of what stuff we are made, or grow to our full stature.

Robert Louis Stevenson (1850–1894), Scottish writer

Shortly after my appointment as health minister and shortly before the 2006 state election, I was advised of a problem at the Berri Hospital in the Riverland. The hospital was in the electorate of Chaffey, held by the sole National Party MP, Karlene Maywald. She supported our minority government and had joined our Cabinet as the Minister for the River Murray. Kid gloves were in order.

Staff at Berri had discovered that a colonoscope had not been properly cleaned since it had been purchased about a year before. As a consequence, more than 200, mostly elderly, people had been potentially exposed to a range of blood-borne viruses, including HIV/AIDS. After a year of use, it was realised the device had two apertures at the 'pointy end', rather than the one on the device that had been replaced. The new aperture was tiny and, it was explained to me, was used to allow the proceduralist to squirt air or water, as required, during examinations. During cleaning a droplet of water had collected at the tiny opening concealing its existence – hence it was never properly cleaned.

I discovered the hospital had not followed its cleaning protocols for over a year – they should have checked their systems multiple times each year. Further, I discovered the manufacturer of the colonoscope had offered training in how to clean the new device but it had been turned down. A failure of clinical and administrative governance had occurred. It gave me no comfort to know that the local elected board was responsible – as was the case for all of our country hospitals. I knew who would have to explain in parliament and in the community.

I acted directly and quickly. I sought advice about my powers under legislation and discovered there was a provision, believed to have been used only once before, which allowed me to direct the board to act. So the CE, Jim Birch, the chief medical officer, Chris Baggoley, my staff and I descended on the hospital where I had summonsed board members and managers to an emergency meeting. After reading them the 'riot act' we set in train the necessary steps to address the issues, including contacting the 200 people who needed to be tested.

After the preparations had been made I issued a press release providing all of the information to the public. I was expecting huge interest. Two hundred elderly people facing AIDS checks! Surprisingly, the matter received only scant coverage – I think only one TV station in Adelaide covered the story. I am certain if we had attempted to cover up what had happened, interest would have been much greater. Fortunately, none of those tested had been affected – despite the anxiety of having to wait quite long periods for the results.

We were lucky on this occasion, but even when things don't go as smoothly early intervention, action and an announcement mean the damage is limited. The bad news in the media is truncated when all the details are revealed up front.

This episode reaffirmed something I had long believed and frequently stated: you don't get judged so much on what happens when you are a minister, but on how you deal with it. A 'crisis' is what happens when the minister doesn't deal effectively, openly and completely with a problem. You have to be decisive – and involved. Generally for operational matters ministers should be at arm's length, but when problems emerge they have to get their hands dirty.

Around the same time as the Berri problem, there was a serious issue involving the serving of cold meats infected with *Listeria monocytogenes* to vulnerable patients in some of our hospitals. Listeria is a common-enough bug found in uncooked meats and soft cheeses. Most of us can consume it with no ill effect. But it can pass across the placenta of pregnant women causing miscarriage or infection of the baby, and those with compromised immune systems, such as cancer patients and the elderly, can become very ill and in some cases die.

In December 2005 public health officials became aware of a number of patients of both public and private hospitals who had become ill from listeria. Over the month we learned that two patients, one of whom died in the previous October, had contracted listeriosis after eating cold meat prepared in the kitchen at the RAH (though one of the patients had died at Gawler Hospital). The strain of listeria was also found in the packaging area of Conroy's smallgoods, which supplied meat to the RAH. Another patient of a private hospital had also died from a different strain of listeriosis.

There was massive media and public interest in this story – but the facts were incredibly complex and difficult to obtain quickly. In particular the incubation period for listeriosis was two to three months – so that meant a long period between the consumption of the contaminated food and symptoms appearing. Who remembers what they ate a week ago, let alone two or three months ago? Making it particularly complex was the fact the patients had been in and out of a variety of hospitals in that time. The work done by the department's experts to work out what had happened, who had eaten what and when, and then to identify possible sources and strains was painstaking and a great example of the incredible calibre of the people working in our public service. These easily lambasted head office bureaucrats.

Despite their good work I felt we were on the back foot the whole time. Why hadn't I warned the public sooner? Why hadn't Conroy's been made to recall its meat products earlier? Why wouldn't I provide the names of the deceased patients? Why was I victimising this South Australian company? The *Advertiser* was particularly virulent in its criticisms – accusing me of secrecy and cover-ups; on Tuesday 13 December running this headline on their front page: 'COVER-UP: Public wasn't alerted to bug threat'.

I tried to explain, without much luck, that legislation prohibited me from handing out information that might reveal an individual's identity; and there were other laws preventing me from identifying Conroy's without due process. The Garibaldi food poisoning case of a decade earlier coloured the way the media and the public viewed this case. There was not much I could do but to make myself available and provide as much information as I could legally and technically.

So, nearly every day for about two weeks, Dr Kevin Buckett, who was in charge of public health, Dr Chris Baggoley the chief medical officer and I would go through the issues with the media. After a few days the words *'Listeria monocytogenes'* rolled off my tongue without the stumbles of the first media conference and I became expert on the testing regimes and incubation process. Eventually, the family of one of the deceased patients was found by the media and the photograph of this poor man (who had been diabetic), was splashed in the *Advertiser* and elsewhere. Eventually details of the second deceased man, a cancer sufferer, were also revealed – but in his case the listeria strain was different.

As with everything this issue passed and the health department substantially reviewed kitchen and food protocols.

What makes health such a stimulating area of responsibility is never knowing what is going to happen next. And while you would never willingly ask for a listeria outbreak or a dirty colonoscope, these issues are challenging to deal with and they put you on your mettle and bring people together. A war-cabinet atmosphere develops around the minister's and CE's offices – early morning meetings, late evening meetings, events cancelled, media conferences called, ministerial statements made – and adrenalin flows.

In the early stages of such an event getting to know the facts becomes the first priority – and that can be difficult. On one occasion we became aware of a man with HIV/AIDS who, contrary to the law, was allegedly actively engaging in unprotected sex with other men he had contacted through the Gaydar website. As a result there had been a spike in the gay community of the strain of HIV/AIDS he carried. This was another difficult case to deal with – huge and salacious community and media interest and the real potential to turn into a witch-hunt. Catherine Hockley, my media advisor, decided to learn more about Gaydar and signed up, under a *nom de plume*. She found out a lot more than she bargained for.

All of the potential crises I faced were different but the need to know the facts in each case was the same. Knowing how a colonoscope is cleaned and how food can be infected with listeria were starting points in dealing with those issues. In the

Gaydar case knowing how that internet pick-up site worked and how it seduced vulnerable men was important. So, too, was understanding how the health system managed such cases. So I visited the RAH sexual health clinic on North Terrace, where the staff members were under pressure as a result of criticisms about how the alleged perpetrator was managed. Many had worked for the service for decades and were among the most dedicated public servants you could meet. They deal on a daily and ongoing basis with the complex health and social issues of people who are vulnerable, or mentally unwell, not very bright or just plain unlucky. Or, in some cases, malicious. I also wanted to show my personal support for the job they do.

As a minister I relished the opportunities of visiting these work sites and learning how things worked. It meant when a problem arose I was better able to explain to the public in simple language what was going on. This was an aim not always achieved.

During the swine flu epidemic the entire national health system went into overdrive to protect our citizens. There was a real fear that many people might die. Epidemiologists kept saying we were due for a really bad epidemic and this might be the one. The planning around 'bird flu' coloured thinking, and certainly the infection and death rates overseas were very concerning. Because our flu season followed that of Europe and North America, we had an advantage in terms of preparation and a vaccine was eventually developed.

A report in the *Australian* (23/7/09) explains the course of the press conference called to announce details of the vaccine:

> South Australian Health Minister John Hill usually has an eloquent yet succinct way with words, but yesterday, as he discussed the new swine flu vaccine being tested by biotech company CSL, the former English teacher borrowed a leaf out of someone else's book: 'The

expectation is that CSL, which produces lots of vaccines, will do this in a way which will have minimal risk but that nonetheless there a are a set of protocols about testing so that those risks are minimised. (Now a short, Strewth-sponsored ad medically advisable intermission. There now back to Hill ...) But you could make a decision at any point along the spectrum once the vaccine has been produced to give it to a particular person if on balance the risks associated with giving it to that person were less than the risks associated with not having tested it properly before giving it to that person.' As the Adelaide media became silent, the penny dropped. Hill conceded: 'Sounds like a Kevin Rudd answer.'

§

The necessity and benefits of being out and about as a minister seem pretty obvious but not all ministers get this. In my first term in parliament (1997–2002) I saw how avoiding this ministerial duty could sink a career. I was the shadow environment minister when there was a biggish oil spill from Esso's Port Stanvac oil refinery. The oil glugged its way south and a lot ended up on Moana Beach, in the heart of my electorate. There was, naturally enough, very strong media and community interest – manna from heaven for any Opposition. I cannot recall what attack line I used against the government – no doubt about the perceived weakness of the EPA and a demand for a proper clean up, which eventually happened.

What I do remember was the failure of the minister, Dorothy Kotz, to heed my call and that of others to visit the beach and see the damage for herself. The issue lasted a week and Dorothy just wouldn't visit, eventually flying to Hobart for a ministerial conference. It looked very bad. I was able to claim that she didn't care and that she had the wrong priorities and I called for her to be dismissed. Shortly afterwards the premier, John Olsen, demoted Dorothy to a less contentious portfolio.

ON BEING A MINISTER

A visit by Dorothy would have given the impression she cared (which she probably did); she would have looked in charge and her career enhanced, rather than damaged. The public doesn't judge a minister on what happens when they are in charge, but how they respond. People are wise; they expect there will be problems and mistakes and breakdowns – what they want is for their minister to take charge and fix the problem.

Shortly after I became environment minister, there was a flood event early one morning at Glenelg, which caused minor damage to a number of homes near the Patawalonga River. As soon as I heard about the flooding I called my driver Paul Adey to collect me and take me there. I wasn't sure of the cause or who was responsible but my instincts told me to go, as it involved infrastructure managed by one of my agencies. I was able to show sympathy, and provide assurances the government would investigate thoroughly and wouldn't desert the residents; all of which was reported by the media along with pictures of flooded houses and interviews with locals, some of whom were upset, others more sanguine.

Pat Conlon, as the minister in charge of SA Water, was given responsibility for managing the issue, with support from my agency. As the insurance companies were a bit sluggish in dealing with claims the government decided to cash-flow individuals, who were growing frustrated at the pace of assistance. I was pleased to inform the community of that at a public meeting.

Pat, as Minister for Emergency Services, was also minister-in-charge when Cabinet drew together all the resources of government to deal with the aftermath of the disastrous 2005 Wangarry bushfire. This was a real crisis. There had been massive destruction and considerable loss of life. I was proud of the way

CHALLENGES

our government did everything it could to help this community to recover and of the regular on-the-ground presence of Premier Mike Rann. As awful as these events are, there is something profoundly inspiring in the way a community comes together to support fellow citizens suffering. This is not a time to be political but a time when real political leadership is needed, as Anna Bligh showed in Queensland during the devastating 2011 floods, which affected so many. Her calm, determined and very human leadership at that critical time saw her popularity soar, but it did nothing to help her survival at the elections held later that year.

The benchmark in how not to deal with a major crisis was shown by George W. Bush in his handling of the Katrina hurricane that devastated so much of New Orleans. His apparent lack of empathy for the victims and the woeful and under-resourced recovery process was a stain on the American character and gave rise to angry responses including the brilliant TV series *Treme*. His remoteness contrasted strongly with his determined and very hands-on response to the 9/11 attacks.

In Australia, in 1974, Cyclone Tracy wiped out Darwin and a lot of Prime Minister Gough Whitlam's remaining credibility. Although the acting PM, Jim Cairns, was on the ground very quickly inspecting the damage and comforting victims, the community wanted to know where our PM was. Unfortunately he was on an extended trip to Europe, which included a highly publicised inspection of ancient ruins. He eventually came home, visited Darwin and then restarted his European tour. This made matters worse. At a time of crisis the public want their leader with them, taking charge, being the focus for grief and hope. This is not something to be delegated. Even though the Darwin recovery program was superb, Gough was never forgiven for his apparent indifference.

In 2008 I received advice that made my heart sink. Tony Sherbon, the health CE, informed me that the RAH's linear accelerators (machines used in the treatment of many cancers), had been incorrectly calibrated between 2004 and 2006. An eventual review found that over 800 patients for at least some of their treatments had been receiving less radiotherapy than was prescribed. The machines were under-dosing by about five per cent. What made this revelation worse, from my point of view, was that the error had been discovered and corrected in 2006 but a clinical decision was made that, as the variation was minor, patients, the public and the minister didn't need to be told. When it was made public the reaction was predictable.

Then, as so often seems to happen, 'sods' law' applied and another cancer-related problem emerged: we became aware of errors in chemotherapy doses provided to children.

As new information came out and anxiety levels grew, the media had a field day. A perfect storm that undermined confidence in the system had been created. The clinicians, of course, were devastated. But like all such issues you can only put them to bed by fully revealing all the information. That meant for me, in this case, learning about how oncology drugs are made and how linear accelerators work. I explained that and then made sure the problems were fixed and everything was being done to make sure they didn't recur.

Inevitably in such cases, an independent and expert review has to be undertaken; then published and enacted. Every step along the way there are great opportunities for Opposition spokespeople to make hay. All the minister can do is be available, factual, calm, reassuring and determined to fix the problem, and be confident that this too will pass. In such cases, I liked to visit

CHALLENGES

the sites where the problems occurred, to both understand what had happened and to reassure anxious staff that they continued to be valued.

I was health minister for so long and was so frequently in the media talking about health issues and often in a technical way, that quite a lot of people assumed I was a doctor myself. But my knowledge was only ever transient.

In my matriculation year, 1967, I studied mostly arts subjects, and double maths, which included calculus. I was able to manage the problems pretty well during the year, but never really understood what calculus was about – until the night before the exam, when a light came on. That knowledge stayed with me until about ten minutes after the exam and has never returned.

This talent for short-term understanding of complex technical issues stood me in good stead as both environment and health minister.

§

The final issue I dealt with as a minister was potentially the most disastrous. BreastScreen SA, a proud and dedicated organisation within SA Health, became aware that following the digitisation of screening equipment the detection rate for potential cancers was lower than predicted.

About 57 per cent of targeted women (50–69 years) regularly have mammograms in SA and as a consequence over 1000 cases of breast cancer are detected each year – many, much earlier than without the screening. As a consequence breast cancer mortality is at an historic low, falling 37 per cent nationally since the program was introduced in 1991. The rate of testing, while below the national target of 70 per cent, is one of the highest in Australia as a result of the assiduous work of the passionate team who work for BreastScreen SA.

However, our performance rate was under pressure from two factors: the ageing of our population, meaning more women in the targeted age group, and the dated technology using traditional wet processing of X-rays which was inefficient and breaking down. I was pleased that after much debate I had been able to convince Cabinet to stump up the extra money to match Commonwealth contributions to digitise the entire system. This was expected to improve productivity and allow the service to cope with the anticipated growth in demand, without extra resources. The then treasurer (and also my successor as health minister), Jack Snelling, and I made the announcement at BreastScreen SA's headquarters on Unley Road in the lead up to the 2011 state Budget. This was a difficult Budget and the announcement was one of the few positives to focus on.

So having identified so closely with the new equipment, I was shocked to learn that detection rates, following the roll out of the new equipment, showed fewer cancers being detected. This only came to light because of the thoroughness of BreastScreen SA's protocols. Nonetheless, it meant that over 53,000 women who had been told that no breast cancer had been detected would now face uncertainty. The stats showed that about 100 cases had been missed; in other words there could be 100 women with breast cancer whose chances of survival may have been reduced. The only comforting advice was that the sizes of the missed cancers were likely to be very small and would have likely been picked up in the next round of screenings.

In discussion with senior clinicians and managers of the

service we identified a range of possible explanations:
1. The technology was at fault. This was considered to be unlikely, as the technology was used widely in Australia and rates had not appeared to fall in other states.
2. Incorrect installation of software. Also considered to be unlikely; by the end of the 18-month data collection period rates had returned to normal.
3. Human error in the reading of the X-rays. Most likely, but still unlikely, given the experience level of the radiologists and the fact they were experienced in reading digital X-rays in their private practices, although from different manufacturers.
4. Statistical anomaly – there were just fewer cancers in that group of women. Nobody believed that – especially as the data showed fewer really small cancers were picked up in the digital testing.

We had a problem. What should we do? One option was to do nothing; as in the case of the under-dosing radiotherapy, the risks were considered minimal. Nobody supported this option.

The officials proposed a scientific re-examination of a large sample of screens – around 10,000 – to try and get a more accurate picture of what had happened. I did not support this option as I believed every woman given what she thought was a clean bill of health would be anxious, and each deserved to know her status as soon as humanly possible. I suggested, and my officers agreed, that we should re-examine all of the screens and randomly choose a selection of 10,000 to assess.

This was an occasion when my political judgement as minister had to override the technical experts. That's why we have ministers running agencies and not technocrats.

So the strategy adopted was to have all of the screens reread by experienced radiologists from other states, starting with the earliest screens. Some of our SA radiologists were strongly opposed to this approach, as they felt their professional integrity was being questioned – they preferred the more cautious and 'scientific' approach. I met with their representatives and told them I understood their concerns but felt the concerns of patients had to come first. As it happened there were no criticisms of the radiologists; indeed, I was pleased to receive a letter from their College congratulating me on the way the issue had been handled.

We knew what we had to do and when and by whom, now we had to decide how to tell the affected women and the public – and we had to act quickly, because once you start dealing with such issues there is always the possibility of a leak. Not necessarily a malicious one, but everyone has a relative or friend who works in health – even journalists; it only takes a someone to overhear a conversation over a meal or glass of wine and the story breaks before you are ready. Loose lips sink ships.

Cynics would say that governments want to hold back bad news stories in order to 'spin' or 'bury' them by announcing them on days when another big story breaks. This does happen, of course. The brilliant TV series *The West Wing* referred to the practice of releasing such stories on Fridays, as Washington prepared for the weekend break, as 'putting out the garbage'. This was not on our agenda with the BreastScreen issue. I knew that any attempt to cover or spin this would have been a disaster. But we did need a good communication strategy so that we could offer information and support to women, who without care might become fearful and panic. Headlines in advance of our managed release stating '50,000 women at risk of cancer', 'Bungled testing fiasco', or 'Secret report leaked' would not only have created a negative political story but also created great anxiety in the community.

Fortunately, it didn't leak and we got together a first-class communication strategy including over 50,000 individual letters, with very detailed Qs and As, one to every woman tested, including those tested on the older analogue system, a phone hotline with trained nurses and doctors available, and extended opening hours for the clinic.

My chief of staff at the time, Dominic Stefanson, remembers the draft documents that came up from the department on this occasion were somewhat defensive and required significant editing by my political staff. The department drafts in such circumstances usually focus on explaining and defending systems and machines – no doubt aimed at protecting both the department and the government – whereas my staff looked at them 'politically'; not in any partisan sense but from the point of view of the person receiving the letter. Dominic, on reading and editing the BreastScreen drafts, kept these questions in mind: What will my mother-in-law think? What questions will she have? My staffers would never question the technical detail, but would have a lot to say about how it was expressed. To them the public was our boss and we needed to account to them honestly, clearly, promptly and comprehensively.

Eventually we were prepared – all that was left was to tell the community, via the media. So on the afternoon of 13 December Dr Gelarah Farshid, the clinical director, and I confronted a full media conference in my conference room on the ninth floor of the health department building. I gave an overview covering all the facts as I knew them: what the risks were, what plans we had to retest, and the information about to be sent to the women involved. I also made the point that it was important women not be deterred from testing; even with this problem they were better off than the 45 per cent of women who had never had a test.

Then Dr Farshid spoke to the media – the first time she had fronted a press conference and she was understandably nervous. But she was sensational with her clear explanations presented confidently. Often in those conferences the media want to dispense with the technical aspects and move quickly into the politics – but not on this occasion. While they gave us both a grilling at the press conference, which went for well over 45 minutes (a long time standing in front of four cameras, bright lights and many ambitious young things wanting to make their career on the basis of how they trapped a minister), there was no angle we hadn't considered or couldn't address.

A couple of days later I visited the BreastScreen clinic to thank and reassure the staff, who felt gutted by the whole event – helping women is all they care about – and to hear about the phone calls. They had received hundreds in the first few days. While a few were nasty the majority were just seeking information and reassurance and most callers thanked the staff for letting them know what was happening. Letters to the editor were equally full of praise for the way it was handled.

If there was any spin it was using the publicity around the case to encourage women who didn't regularly have breast screening to do so. And a potential political disaster became an exemplar of how to manage a challenging issue and avoid a crisis.

In late May 2013, my successor as health minister Jack Snelling released the report into the investigations to a full media

CHALLENGES

conference and appropriately accepted responsibility on behalf of the government. He apologised and explained that helping the women whose cancer had been missed was his top priority, and that the government would act as a 'model litigant' in any subsequent legal action. The Opposition shadow minister looked irrelevant calling for yet another inquiry; the only negative media interest was generated by lawyers building their 'class action' case. Interestingly, following the report's release, letters to the editor were once again generally supportive.

At about the same time that this issue arose then minister for education, Grace Portolesi, commissioned Justice Debelle to enquire into the handling of a truly shocking sexual assault on a seven-year-old girl by an out-of-school-hours-care worker in 2010. The inquiry focused on the management of communications around the issue and not the legal proceedings against the perpetrator, who was arrested, pleaded guilty, was convicted and gaoled – all in good time. This case is a classic example of how not to manage an issue, which went on to dominate parliament, the media and the community for much of 2013 – all because full disclosure had not happened in 2010.

What drove the matter was the persistence of a member of the school governing council who demanded that parents be informed. The particular parent, who worked professionally as a police investigator, quite reasonably believed that parents should be given the facts, in part to determine whether other children had been abused, in part to counter the rumours circulating, and also because of a belief that parents had a right to know.

The Debelle Report found that the Education Department had made a series of poor decisions based on a false belief that they were legally prevented from disclosing information to parents. It also emerged that Jay Weatherill, as education minister in 2010, was not briefed on the issue, despite emails to his staff about it. Grace Portolesi, who inherited the portfolio after the prosecution had been completed, was left to carry the political can, and following wrong advice from her department gave inaccurate information to parliament. As a consequence of these failures, an awful matter occurring in 2010, which could have been dealt with cleanly at that time, was still making headlines in 2013. It meant that the victim's family and the school community generally were unable to move on, and it also led to Grace losing her position as education minister and several senior education department officials leaving their jobs. The politics were awful: it looked like a cover-up was in place, the department and government looked incompetent, and of course there was plenty for a cynical Opposition to exploit.

For me the breast screening issue finished off 2012 pretty much as it began. If ever I had an *annus horribilis* it was 2012. From the beginning of the year a huge number of issues converged to occupy me and my office with damage control. This was capitalised on by the shadow minister Martin Hamilton-Smith, who, very effectively, was using health as a platform to mount an attack on the Liberal leadership – an attack that eventually failed. But health gave him plenty of opportunities to get attention in 2012. Like all shadows he constructed an argument that the individual matters grouped together demonstrated a crisis, a crisis that, he argued, was beyond my capacity to deal with. Ironically, Marty now serves as an independent minister in the Labor Government, formed following the very close 2014 state election.

There was certainly a lot to deal with – especially the

management of unrealistic budget targets, a very bad auditor-general's report (providing massive ammunition for the Opposition), and then claims about ramping.

'Ramping' is used to describe the practice used in most states of Australia to manage patients in ambulances on ED ramps when the emergency departments are too busy to accept the patients – who are instead managed in ambulances by ambulance paramedics. This is done as a matter of policy in most states as a way of managing ED pressure. It was not and had never been the policy of the SA Government. The turnaround time covers the movement of the patient into the ED, the handover to the nurse on duty, paperwork, and the clean up of the ambulance ready for another patient. The goal is to have all of this done within 30 minutes, but there are plenty of good reasons – none of them associated with ramping – why this can take longer; sometimes a blow-out can occur because the paramedic goes to the toilet or has something to eat before getting back on the road. Hospitals routinely record these times and report on them.

A regular topic of my media interviews during my last few years as health minister was the concern about ambulance turnaround times, especially at Flinders Medical Centre. The issue was usually brought to the attention of the media without advance notice to the health system, or me, by the ambulance union or one or two of its more militant members. A photograph of a line-up of ambulances (often empty and parked while ambos had breaks) might accompany the story. Claims would be made that the critically ill were made to wait for very long periods in the back of an ambulance. The lack of notice, before being asked by the media to comment, made these claims difficult to address.

At the heart of the problem was the lack of a common view

between FMC ED staff and SAAS officers about what should happen when the pressure was on. In most other hospitals there would be a common-sense response. During my term the Flinders ED was considerably refurbished and its capacity expanded. During this reconstruction I expressed the view that issues of ambulance-to-hospital transfers would be fixed once the development was completed. Unfortunately, the design (strongly influenced by ED clinicians) included a relatively small waiting space – forcing the de facto implementation of a policy to ramp patients in ambulances once the waiting room was full. This was defended by the ED clinicians who argued that this was the best way to manage surges. The ambos disputed this – they wanted to drop off patients and get back on the road as quickly as possible.

The dispute was really about power; it infuriated me that two elements of the one system (ED staff and SAAS officers) were fighting each other in a public way. Eventually, the head of the ED took leave and an outside ED specialist was brought in to produce recommendations to settle the issue. The irony was that FMC was transferring patients on average more quickly than other hospitals – but the perception was the reverse.

§

One of the many critical issues examined closely by the auditor-general (which made 2012 such a difficult year) was the department's procurement and implementation of the Oracle IT system.

Oracle is an excellent program for managing complex financial systems across a large multi-faceted organisation such as SA Health. It was introduced to replace over a dozen so-called 'legacy' systems used by various formerly semi-independent parts of SA Health. These legacy systems were breaking down, didn't 'talk' to each other, and were expensive to run. The case to replace them with a single enterprise system was overwhelming.

However as the auditor-general found in his excoriating analysis, published in early 2012, the implementation of the system was highly problematic. This was because the business case was seriously flawed. On the one hand it overestimated the speed at which savings could be made and on the other it assumed that the program could be implemented virtually cost-free. Experience showed that it took a lot longer to implement than was predicted and the savings, though real, would be longer term than expected. What was overlooked was the expensive and time-consuming preparation and training of the staff who had to use it. The so-called 'culture change' process was ignored when developing the business case.

On analysing the problem, following the auditor-general's report, it became clear what had happened. The finance section in the department knew a new system was needed, but there was a view that if all the real costs were included Treasury – and therefore Cabinet – wouldn't approve the necessary allocation. The way the business case was constructed meant that it was virtually cost neutral – but clearly (and with the benefit of hindsight) this was never going to happen in the approved timeframe. What is annoying is that even with the real costs taken into account this project will save money in the longer term.

It is easy to point to flaws in the way SA Health developed the business case and the weak structure in place (rectified in the light of this case going haywire) that allowed it to proceed. However, the underlying problem was one of culture; good public servants believed that unless they squeezed the costs the project would not get up, the systems would ultimately fail, and a greater disaster would then unfold.

Replacement of ageing infrastructure, whether it's in the area of technology, buildings or roads, is always hard for government. It's easier to promote a new project in the community and thus in the media and Cabinet than it is to argue for the replacement of something outdated. When budgets are squeezed often maintenance is the first to be cut. You don't see it in the short term, but the next generation will, just as this generation sees the lack of past maintenance now in our schools and hospitals, and on our roads. The view has developed that you build, only minimally maintain, and then wait for growing pressure to undertake a major renovation, or abandon and rebuild.

For instance, in 2013, with land and improvements valued at more than $3 billion, SA Health was allocated just over $12 million in the state Budget for minor works. A truly insignificant sum compared to the overall capital investment budget for health of $328 million – the vast majority of which was allocated for new developments. Many of these developments, of course, were necessary because of a lack of proper maintenance over decades; and as a government we were playing very expensive 'catch-up'.

Avoiding this cycle is one of the great advantages of the Public Private Partnership (PPP) process. It forces government to assess and budget for the life-cycle costs of whatever is being built. For example, the PPP contract for the New RAH covers a 35-year period and covers the construction costs ($1.85 billion) and importantly the maintenance and replacement costs across the first 30 years of operation. Short-term aspirations to cut costs by reducing maintenance are avoided by this contract.

CHALLENGES

If the state had built the hospital via the more traditional procurement process, it would look great for the first few years then over time it would deteriorate because allocations for maintenance would never cover the real costs.

The Liberals, in Opposition, loved to criticise the New RAH project at every opportunity and would misuse these figures to suggest the project was more expensive than it really was. In truth it is a good deal for the state, and it guarantees that future governments can't cheat and run down the maintenance program for short-term budget benefit. In reality, through this project the state gets two brand-new hospitals – one in 2016, when the New RAH is opened, and another in 2046 at the end of the PPP contract when the hospital is handed to the state in 'as new' condition.

I raise the case of Oracle to show the pitfalls of decision-making in relation to complex matters. Even with a thorough process including internal department processes, review by other government agencies, and a full Cabinet process, a vital element was ignored: preparing staff for the change.

As mentioned, in my view, the public judges governments, not so much as what goes wrong on their watch, but how they respond. Do they cover up? Spin? Blame others? Or face the issues head on and fix them. While the public might allow one such error, if you repeat it you are sunk. We did get Oracle back on track, fixed the internal health system for overseeing IT projects, and made sure in relation to other technology initiatives that the lessons learned were applied.

PARTY

Too bad that all the people who know how to run the country are busy driving taxicabs and cutting hair.

George Burns (1896–1996), US comedian

I voted for the first time in 1960; I was ten years old and in fifth class at Artarmon Public School on Sydney's North Shore. Our estimable teacher, Kelvin Leitch, informed us at the beginning of the school year that he would conduct elections for various class positions, including class captain. And without allocating any time for campaigning or reflection he did just that. It became apparent very quickly that the class had formed itself into two parties: the Boys' Party and the Girls' Party and as there were more girls than boys, the Girls' Party was winning all the positions.

Fortunately for the Boys' Party, the balloting was interrupted by the morning break giving the boys time to develop a strategy to break the stranglehold of the girls. Before the break there were only two candidates for each position: one boy and one girl; each nominated by their own gender. After the break, three nominations would be made for each position – including, shockingly, a second girl nominated by a boy! This stratagem split the Girls' Party vote and ensured some Boys' Party victories. It worked for a while until the girls cottoned on and rejected the second nominations.

I learned two valuable lessons from this experience: firstly, in politics it's all about the numbers, and secondly, there is more than one way to obtain those numbers.

On election night 2002, Nick Minchin and I were part of the ABC Tally Room panel with Kerry O'Brien. Nick, then a Liberal Senator, and I provided the political points of view and the balance. We knew each other pretty well from our days as officials for our respective parties, we both had law degrees and had both moved to Adelaide from Sydney years before. Nick was the only Liberal to send me a note of congratulations when I announced I was retiring from politics. I always found him to be an honest and honourable opponent.

I said at the start of the night that I was pretty certain we would secure 23 of the 47 seats needed to win government, and that it would be a hunt for the 24th – but there were options. And that's exactly how the night ended – we had 23 seats, the Liberals had 20 and there were four independents elected: Bob Such, a former Liberal minister, Rory McEwan, a former Liberal who had supported the Liberals in the last parliament, Karlene Maywald, the sole National member, who had also supported the Liberal Government, and the former Liberal and maverick Peter Lewis. I maintained the line during the night that one of these members might support Labor to form government. Nick scoffed at the idea and pointed out the Liberal credentials of each of the members and the conservative nature of their electorates.

History shows that following weeks of discussions and negotiations Peter Lewis decided to support Labor. What Nick possibly knew in his heart, but couldn't or wouldn't admit, was that the enmity between certain Liberals and Lewis was such that our chances of an agreement were pretty good.

The relationship between Labor and Lewis started off solidly enough but it became clear that the reasons the Liberals and Lewis had fallen out so badly were not all on the one side. Mike Rann moved to consolidate our position very quickly and eventually all four Liberal-leaning independent MPs were supporting the government – indeed McEwan and Maywald both became members of Cabinet in a unique and popular coalition. There were a few mutterings on the Labor side about this alliance but pragmatism prevailed. Mike said that although he led a minority government he intended to govern as though he had a majority of ten. And he did. There is more than one way of getting the numbers.

It is illuminating to compare our 2002 minority government, which was so politically successful we were re-elected with a big swing in 2006, with the minority Gillard Government elected in 2010. Sure the circumstances are different but the contrast is very stark. In many ways the federal Labor Government was a good government – providing strong financial policy that saw Australia survive deadly international economic times, while introducing the national disability insurance scheme, major reforms to education, and a price on carbon. But it was woeful politically. Good at government; bad at politics. And Julia Gillard faced an Opposition leader in Tony Abbott who is without peer in terms of politics.

As a non-factional member of Caucus I owed my position in shadow Cabinet to the support of the leader. As Party secretary I had developed a productive working relationship with Mike Rann and I was grateful for his support in 1997 when I joined the Caucus. Being non-aligned in politics, at whatever level, is a difficult path – if you are not careful both sides will end up distrusting you.

This was the case for one very bright member of the Bannon

Caucus, who during a contest for the deputy leadership position pledged his support to both candidates. What he didn't realise was that the two candidates, Jack Wright and Hugh Hudson, were mates and had agreed that if the numbers were clear there would be no contest. The two sat down and shared their pledged votes and so became quickly aware of the Janus; Jack Wright, I think, phoned the dual pledger and invited him to his office. When he arrived he was confronted by the two rivals and his own calumny. Despite his obvious talent and political skill, the fact he couldn't be trusted meant he was passed over for promotion for years. It must have been galling for him to see lesser lights being elevated to the ministry.

When you are a member of a faction these kinds of choices generally are easy – which candidate is in my faction? I'll vote for him/her. The other fact of factional life, when it is as civilised as it has been in SA Labor politics for many years, is that there are very few Caucus contests. The factions share positions and determine through their internal voting systems whose turn it is to be promoted or dumped. Usually, the leader and the other factional leaders are consulted. This may not be pure democracy – but it is a highly pragmatic means to ensure harmony and make government work.

Political parties obsessed with their own internal workings cannot govern effectively. Labor in SA may have disappointed people and made mistakes, but with a few exceptions, since coming to government in the mid 1960s, Labor has shown great internal discipline and capacity to govern. The community has rewarded that with 37 years of office compared to the 13 years given to a Liberal Party riven by internal schisms and personality battles.

All of the various elements that have made Labor good at

governing – factional discipline, centralised policy making, professional campaigning – have also made joining and participating in the Party seem irrelevant and meaningless to many of our supporters. After every election defeat or near defeat at a state and federal level a few senior members of the Party are appointed to conduct a review. These reviews always say much the same things about broadening participation; recommendations largely ignored in the pragmatic light of day. If we are to have a Party of relevance, we will have to make substantial changes in the areas of structure, power and participation.

The current sub-branch structure has monthly meetings with guest speakers and formal agendas attended by very few of our increasingly shrinking membership base. Our structure was developed before electricity and literacy were widespread and is as relevant to modern political organisation and action as the vow of obedience is to contemporary marriage. We have to change the way we engage and organise our membership locally and nationally. Social media will play an important part but cannot replace face-to-face engagement. How we relate to each other and when and where must change.

When I joined the Party, over 97 per cent of the voting power was held by union affiliates – over time that has fallen to half; while it's unimaginable to have a Labor Party without affiliated unions, as they now cover just eight per cent of the workforce their power has to be reduced even further.

One way to share this power and increase participation would be to allow all members the opportunity to vote in more ballots. At the moment individual sub-branch members can vote in preselection ballots for their local candidate. Frequently having factional agreements in place means that in practice few ballots occur. I would like to see all our members voting in multiple position ballots including those for candidates for the Legislative Council and Senate, and our state executive. This would give all members a stake in outcomes.

As a non-factional member of Caucus I didn't get the chance, often, to express my non-factional opinion by way of a vote. Generally, the number of nominees for a Caucus position equalled the number of positions.

There were two occasions though where I had to choose and where pressure was applied by both sides to support their candidate. Unlike most others in Caucus I didn't have the cover of factional membership and I felt exposed and at risk. A false move could have damaged my career, which relied not on factional preferment but the leader's protection, the consent of Caucus, and my own contributions and skills. Both contests occurred after elections and were for the position of deputy premier. High stakes.

The first ballot happened after the 2002 election when the deputy's position was vacant because our pre-election deputy, Annette Hurley, had vacated her safe seat of Napier for Michael O'Brien and contested, unsuccessfully, the marginal seat of Light. There were two candidates: Kevin Foley and Patrick Conlon. Kevin from the right and Pat from the left. Although it was a civilised contest – Pat and Kevin were good mates and had worked together very effectively in Opposition to bully and bludgeon and bloody a series of Liberal frontbenchers – the contest was serious. It was probably more about how power should be shared than personality or talent. The left believed they deserved someone in a leadership role – the right already had Paul Holloway as leader in the Legislative Council. Mike Rann, like me, was factionally unaligned, though unlike me he had never been in a faction. And I, like Kevin Foley, had been in the Centre-Left until it imploded but unlike him had stayed unaligned.

So how was I to vote? I found the choice a hard one as I knew both Pat and Kevin very well and I didn't want to disappoint either. I was also worried that if I voted one way or the other I would be seen as a de facto member of that person's faction. I was also aware of the damage that could be done to me if I prevaricated and flirted with both. I had to decide, announce my choice, and live with it. In the end I supported Pat, even though knowing, as he did, that Kevin would win anyway. In part I voted for Pat because I bought the line about shared leadership positions; but mostly because politically I felt closer to the left than the right and if I ever felt forced to join a faction I would choose the left. For me the vote for Patrick was insurance. Bizarrely, Patrick eventually broke ranks with the left and while not joining the right went on to enjoy their support.

The second contest for deputy happened after the 2010 election – a weird election swamped by a full-blown Liberal dirty tricks campaign focused on bizarre claims about Mike's personal life. Nonetheless, despite reeling from what felt like a near loss, we were re-elected quite comfortably (in seats if not in votes). The day after the election when we were taking a collective deep breath, I received an early morning phone call from Jay Weatherill letting me know he intended to contest the deputy's position. He reasoned, quite correctly, that the election result showed great dissatisfaction with the style of the government – we were seen as arrogant and non-consultative. Kevin Foley copped, in the public mind, a lot of the responsibility for that. Jay proposed a different way, 'debate and decide' rather that 'announce and defend' – a catchy way of summing up the concerns of voters and presenting an alternative approach.

Jay's move was gutsy and clever. He was signalling that he was the future and had the 'ticker' to do the hard things. His timing meant he couldn't be accused of hurting our election chances and, as after every election all positions are declared automatically vacant, he wasn't technically challenging the incumbent.

After a number of calls with Jay, Kevin and Mike I let Jay know I wouldn't be supporting him but that I would support him for leader when that position came up. I told both Kevin and Mike the same thing. Kevin was pleased with my support for the deputy post, but a little disappointed about the future. I think at that stage he still harboured ambitions to take over from Mike. A couple of years before at 'the night of the long drinks', a Caucus dinner held in Parliament House, Kevin had a rush of blood and declared he was ready to lead. Despite it being laughed off with the hangover, Mike Rann certainly believed it to be true, as he took the time to ring me about it, suggesting I too might be in for the chop.

I remember saying to Jay after the 2006 election that I thought he would be the next leader and I would support him to achieve that. This is despite, or perhaps because of, the fact some saw me as the next Labor premier. Jay told me on several occasions he would support me if I wanted to lead.

My attitude to that was not based on a false modesty (I thought I could do the job) or fear of the responsibility (I've always enjoyed the responsibilities of office) but rather a sober assessment of my own circumstances. I am a few years older than Mike Rann and would turn 64 by the 2014 election – the first one the new premier would face – so it would be hard to present me as the new face of Labor. And I knew by 2010 my ambitions for politics were waning – I was looking forward to getting out altogether, not working harder. In fact, prior to the 2006 election I had decided to make it my last election – however, once I had jumped that hurdle the decision to retire in 2010 seemed premature and after discussions with Andrea I decided to stick around for one more term.

There was a moment though during the lead-up to the 2010 elections – when the Michelle Chantelois allegations aired – when I thought I might have become leader. If Mike had decided to resign I could see the Caucus turning to me – which was confirmed by former Speaker and member for Giles, Lyn Breuer. Mike, of course, was never going to stand down – his resilience is extraordinary and nobody was going to push him just before an election. I was relieved.

After the 2010 election it became clear there were only two realistic candidates for premier when Mike stood down – a move expected sometime in the middle of the term. They were Jay and John Rau, who had finally joined Cabinet as attorney-general after eight years as a bored and disenchanted backbencher.

As a non-factional member I was able to occupy a useful place in the ecology of the Party and Caucus. When the factions experienced difficulty in their dealings with each other, or when neutrality was required, I was sometimes asked to play the honest broker role. So, in Caucus, I was often asked to be the returning officer in ballots for committee positions or highly sought after CPA (Commonwealth Parliamentary Association) trips. In Opposition, when the Party was riven by a branch-stacking outbreak, I was asked by the Party executive to chair a committee to review the Party's rules to eliminate the practice, which we did.

So, partly on my own initiative and partly following a request from Tom Koutsantonis, I tried to help the transition. There were two key issues to be resolved: who would take over and when?

Mike had made it reasonably clear that he wanted to move on and at about the halfway mark – March 2012 – when he would have reached 10 years as premier.

The left was clear who they wanted: Jay Weatherill. The right was in a state of great uncertainty – Kevin Foley? Jack Snelling? John Rau?

Jay was clear how he wanted it to be resolved – he wanted Mike to endorse him as his successor, with the support of the Party and following Kevin's resignation as deputy. Jay would take on that role and that of treasurer, as stepping stones to the big job – in retrospect the ideal way to proceed. However, there were considerable hurdles to clear.

Principally, at this stage the right (or large sections) couldn't stand the thought of a left-wing leader, especially Jay whose positioning had really pissed them off. They did, however, recognise he was popular in the community – and the right, if nothing else, is pragmatic, and they enjoy office.

In reality, the right was divided between John Rau, an urbane moderate low-key option; and Jack Snelling, more dynamic, but also more conservative and harder to sell to the majority of Caucus.

I was convinced the right would eventually support Jay because he offered the best chance to win a fourth term, and as they worked through the options this became clear to their key members as well.

I advised Mike that I thought Jay would and should be his replacement and encouraged him to endorse him as well; the three of us even had a meeting to discuss how it might work, but made little progress.

I also said that while I supported Jay I thought John Rau would be an acceptable leader. And that either combination –

Weatherill/Rau or Rau/Weatherill – would work, we just needed to decide and get on with it. While being second fiddle was obviously not Jay's preference he would have accepted what the numbers dictated. Either way I thought it made sense to put Jay into the deputy's position when Kevin resigned.

At this stage, while the right was warming to Jay, they were reluctant to see him become deputy and treasurer so I suggested the two roles be split: the right would keep Treasury, Jay become deputy. They loved the idea of splitting the roles, although not in the way I envisaged but because it gave them a way, in the short term, to manage their own division. So John Rau became deputy and Jack Snelling treasurer.

It was clear by then that Snelling was out of the race and the leadership contest would be a showdown between Rau and Weatherill. Making Rau deputy made things easier in the short term but more complex later. It certainly made Mike's position more difficult. It appeared the right, by appointing John as his deputy, were telling him John Rau was their preferred candidate. And naturally enough Mike supported John, especially as, following Jay's post-election attempt to become his deputy, there was little love lost between the two.

While I think John Rau would have been a fine premier I preferred Jay Weatherill for a number of reasons, including his intention to do things differently. What persuaded me was that he wanted it more. Ambition is a powerful motivator – the really successful leaders are driven and, as history demonstrates, often slightly mad as well. Rob Kerin, who had taken over as Liberal premier after John Olsen fell on his sword, was a nice bloke but not driven to win and hold the job like Olsen and Rann. This was another reason I dealt myself out. I just didn't want it that much. But Jay did.

Eventually Jay confided in me that the right had come in behind him. I knew by then that Mike was planning to go in March 2012. I tried, unsuccessfully, to convince Jay to support this timetable. In fact, before I became aware of Mike's intentions I had put the argument to Jay that taking over later optimised his and the government's re-election chances. I was thinking of the unexpected loss by the Brumby Labor Government in Victoria. I was surprised it had been Brumby's first campaign as premier – he had taken over from Steve Bracks so soon after the previous election that any freshness had been lost. Every new leader gets a bounce and I calculated that a late changeover from Mike to Jay would maximise the political benefits of that bounce.

Jay believed that by late in the term the government was in the doldrums, voters had stopped listening to Mike and Jay needed time to turn matters around. A reasonable analysis.

In the end, on a Friday evening, the last day of July 2011 and just before he was to open a major British contemporary exhibition at the Art Gallery, Mike was 'tapped'. Two leaders of the right, Jack Snelling and Peter Malinauskas (the young, capable and thoughtful secretary of the shop assistants' union – the right's engine and control centre) told Mike the right was now behind Jay and it wanted change immediately.

This caught Mike by surprise and made him exceptionally and justifiably angry. Following a series of phone calls and meetings between key players, a more nuanced transfer was arranged – Mike and Jay eventually held a press conference together, announcing the transition would occur in October 2011, allowing Mike to complete some key projects and announcements.

It could have been handled better; but compared to many

leadership transfers, for example Rudd to Gillard or any of the state's Liberal coups, it was reasonably bloodless.

As a senior minister, a non-factional player, former Labor secretary and a confidante to both men, I tried to smooth the transition. For much of this period I felt awful, heavy in my heart and anxious. I hate conflict. My parents had a highly fraught marriage full of conflict, a stressed and anxious environment to grow up in. As the elder of two children I felt responsible and took on the role of peacemaker.

In politics I relish the conflict of ideas, debate about policy, and the hurly-burly of day-to-day engagement. What I hated was the political equivalent of a 'domestic'. That's what the leadership battle felt like to me – so I was compelled to get involved to resolve it.

My first campaign, in 1982: 'Mitcham – an UpHill Battle'. I'd even had a haircut and beard trim in preparation.

Before I was elected in 1997 I had this photo taken of Andrea, our sons Eric (front) and Luke, and Andrea's parents Mavis and Ron for an election pamphlet. Unfortunately, because of the sharp wind and sun in our eyes none of us looked happy. The photo was never used.

I enjoyed being environment minister, as this picture, taken in 2003 with local mayor Ray Gilbert and environmentalist David Suzuki at the opening of the Willunga Farmers' Market, shows. *[Courtesy Fleurieu Photographics]*

Graham Gunn (right) was my favourite MP from the other side. I was pleased to join him and Lynn Brake, chairman of the Arid Areas Water Catchment board, at Mungerannie in his vast northern electorate in 2003. *[Courtesy Fleurieu Photographics]*

At my first Health Ministers' meeting, in 2005, with then Commonwealth Minister for Health Tony Abbott.

We liked to celebrate good news. Here, just before the 2006 state election.

Campaigning in 2007 with then Opposition Leader Kevin Rudd, Nicola Roxon, and current member for Kingston Amanda Rishworth at Noarlunga Hospital.

The *Advertiser* photographer set me up beautifully with the help of the Adelaide hip hop band Hilltop Hoods. *[Courtesy* Advertiser *newspaper]*

I loved speaking at Fringe and Cabaret Festival openings, where the audience was primed to laugh at even the worst 'dad' joke.

My predilection to return to my teacherly ways often came to the fore in Question Time. *[Courtesy* Advertiser *newspaper]*

With my Country Health plan I was able to achieve something the Liberals had been failing at for years – unite rural South Australia against the government.
[*Courtesy* Advertiser *newspaper*]

My staff were talented and loyal. Posing here with four chiefs of staff: (from left) Catherine Hockley, Chris Picton, Kym Winter-Dewhirst and Brer Adams, c. 2007.

Posing at Tony Sherbon's and Catherine Hockley's wedding: (from left) Chris Picton, Brer Adams, me, Catherine, Health CE Tony, and Dominic Stefanson.

The *Advertiser* used this photograph in 2009 to illustrate my distress over the first death from swine flu; in reality my mind was miles away.
[Courtesy Advertiser *newspaper]*

Signing the contract in 2010 for the new Royal Adelaide Hospital, one of the biggest social infrastructure projects in Australia's history.

This highly unflattering photograph was used by the *Advertiser* in 2012 to show I was 'under pressure'.
[Courtesy Advertiser *newspaper]*

The Save the RAH party invested a lot of money and time for poor electoral results – but they certainly had a big impact in the lead-up to the 2010 election.
[Courtesy Advertiser *newspaper]*

I found Twitter a great way to communicate and find out what was happening. This 'selfie' taken accidentally at a Tour Down Under event became my avatar.

I was the first minister in Australia to use an iPad for Cabinet documents. Showing it here, in 2010, to colleagues Paul Caica, Jack Snelling and Tom Koutsantonis.
[Courtesy Advertiser *newspaper]*

South Australia received the Dirty Ashtray Award from the AMA in 2010 for being the worst performing state in tobacco control. We were pleased to turn it around, receiving the award for best performing state in 2011 from AMA President Peter Sharley (right), and CEO Joe Hooper.

David Panter, an outstanding public servant, drove the New RAH project.

In the art centre at Amata with senior artist Hector Burton. I liked to visit the APY Lands each year to remind myself what life there was like and what was needed.

Having my blood pressure taken in Rundle Mall by the secretary of the Australian Nursing and Midwifery Federation, Liz Dabars, on International Nurses Day, c. 2011.

Mike Rann's last Question Time as premier – smiling on the outside as he passes on the mantle to Jay Weatherill. I am in my usual position – the middle.
[Courtesy Advertiser *newspaper]*

An essential part of the job – tough media conferences. Here with Premier Jay Weatherill at Lyell McEwin Hospital.

With two beautiful apple munchers at an OPAL (Obesity Prevention and Lifestyle) event, c. 2012.

Pointing out the state's previous health ministers to Ruth Awbery. I was the 15th and second longest serving after Lyell McEwin, who clocked up 26 continuous years – a record unlikely to be broken.

My last day as minister, with Deb Pow who ran my electorate office and Carolyn Lee who ran my ministerial office.

In January 2013, after 11 years, it was time for my driver Paul Adey and I to part.

My staffers tended to be academics, journalists and lawyers. (From left to right) Paula Furby, Ruth Awbery, me, Leah Manuel, Dominic Stefanson and Anita Ewing in 2013. Paula and Dominic have PhDs; Ruth and Leah worked in the media; and Anita is a lawyer.

As prime minister, Bob Hawke was a brilliant advocate. Pictured here with Douglas Gautier, CE of the Adelaide Festival Centre, in 2013.

I was always grateful that Andrea was prepared to be my 'plus one' at important events. *[Courtesy Solstice Media]*

9

PARLIAMENT

Parliament will train you to talk; and above all things to hear, with patience, unlimited quantities of foolish talk.

Thomas Carlyle (1795–1881), Scottish philosopher

All ministers, in addition to their portfolio duties, share the responsibility for ensuring that government works. Each minister brings to that role the skills, talents, and attitudes honed from their time in politics and from outside political life. In addition to the role of peacemaker, I felt my time as a teacher contributed to my work as minister.

Mike Rann was a former journalist and he brought that set of skills to the job, as the name 'Media Mike' attests. In parliament, the media and speeches he was great at delivering the one-line grab. He used to say he looked for the headline in every story and event. This was effective at driving his point home. You were never unsure of Mike's position; there was no grey. Of course, this could also be seen as rehearsed, or slick and insincere.

This is Mike in a ministerial statement on 20 November 2007 on one of his favourite topics:

> The government has today announced the next phase of comprehensive laws designed to disrupt and dismantle criminal bikie gangs. These are the toughest anti-outlaw bikie gang laws that we can find anywhere in the world where these gangs operate.

On the Finks Motorcycle Club:

> I will not now, nor will I ever, apologise for the strong action this government has taken to assist the police in tackling organised crime gangs ... Of course, the Liberals did not want Spencer Von Einem to be DNA tested; whenever there is some dirty crim, we see their civil liberties being defended by members opposite. (3 February 2009)

On uranium mining on 20 April 2008:

> We have seen a tenfold increase in mining exploration under this government compared to when the Liberals were in power, because they were anti-mining and anti-development. Someone had to have the guts to change the policy and embrace uranium mining – and it might as well have been me. I know that I am referred to as Yellowcake Rann around the place, but I am happy to live with that ...

Here Mike demonstrated not only the sharpness of his expression, but also his sense of humour; all members knew that Mike, as a young man, made his mark as an anti-nuke campaigner.

Jay Weatherill, on the other hand, as a former lawyer, tends to provide the facts, weigh them up and provide a considered position; a 'on the one hand and on the other hand' approach. This means that while Jay comes over as sincere and measured, he can seem more discursive than decisive. Where Mike was more interested in outcome, Jay seems more interested in process. Where Mike delivered headlines, Jay delivers editorials. 'Debate and decide', rather than 'announce and defend'.

On 18 September 2012, Jay delivered a ministerial statement on the public sector:

> This is a serious matter for public debate but, like all serious debate, it should proceed from a common understanding of the facts. As at 30 June 2011 ... there were 101,485 people employed, or 84,882 full-time equivalents; and 33,537 of those full-time equivalents were

police, doctors, nurses and teachers ... So when cuts of up to 35,000 people from the public sector are foreshadowed, the community needs to appreciate that this necessarily means cuts to the group of workers who we rely on in times of need.

In releasing an Economic Statement, Jay told the House on 16 October 2012:

Throughout the history of South Australia our economic development has been based on a shared vision of the future that has been supported by a strong consensus across the community. From the dreams of a planned settlement in a 19th-century English drawing room to the industrialisation of our state under Sir Thomas Playford ... little about our economic development has happened by chance ... the government will produce a new economic statement for South Australia ... The first part of this process is laying out the government's vision ...

Even when it came to his dramatic plan to ban 'live odds' betting during televised sport, Jay was still very measured in his language when he informed parliament that

South Australian families have become increasingly frustrated about the penetration of gambling advertising into sporting coverage ... The state government will not be willing to sit back and allow live odds advertising to become an integral part of Australian sport.

The public generally, and some might say perversely, seems to prefer the opposite approach to the one on offer. When one of the most decisive politicians of modern times, Jeff Kennett, was premier of Victoria he generated huge anger and protest and was eventually turfed out by the genial Steve Bracks. The next Liberal premier, Ted Bailleu, was dumped by his party for not being decisive enough. An opinion reflected in poor poll numbers.

Pat Conlon, who was a lawyer (and is again), was also in his youth a waterside worker. His approach, particularly in debate, is a unique combination of the skills developed in both these careers, grafted on to a naturally witty point of view. Patrick could be brutal in parliament – bringing together his sharp legal mind and love of language with the brute force of a punch-up.

On 29 September 2010, in response to a question on the Adelaide Oval development, Pat had this to say:

> *'I tried to be polite, that didn't work, so I am not going to do that this time.'*

(Mitch Williams interjects)

> *'Go and find a friend and leave me alone, will you? Go and find a friend, mate ...'*

(Members interject)

> *'Actually I was losing my sleep. I was worrying whether the member for Unley would believe me, but he believes in lots of things. He is a very easy person to get to believe in things; we remember those documents. He picked them up. They were full of Seventh-day Adventists and shady deals; he said, "This has got to be true."'*

John Rau was appointed in 2010 to the frontbench and quickly made his mark with his somewhat droll approach as seen in this contribution to a debate on wind energy. He was addressing the comments made by a number of MPs that the jury is still out on the health effects of wind turbines, even though the evidence shows there are no health effects, other than what were described in one scientific paper as 'nocebo' effects. That is, residents become anxious and thus ill as a result of their exposure to all of the campaigning.

Rau:

> *It reminded me of something that happened to me personally when I was taking my children to Falls Creek a few years ago. We arrived at*

> Mount Beauty in a bus. The bus driver ... as we were driving up the hill, says over the microphone, 'Ladies and gentlemen, a person on this bus a week or so ago counted 372 turns from here to the top of the mountain,' and we start going up. About a kilometre up, he says, 'And ladies and gentlemen, pretty soon some of you might start feeling ill,' and then he hands the plastic bags to the people in the bus and says, 'Pass them on. Anyone who wants to vomit, please grab one of these bags.' Sure enough within about four minutes, a lady who was sitting just across from me felt the urge and the predictable happened, and then my children had the same problem, and there was an epidemic of it in the bus. The only person who was not affected was me and, unfortunately, that meant I had to collect the bags. The point is: that is what is going on with wind farms. (Hansard, 20 March 2013)

As a former teacher I tend to want to educate my audience. I will give them the facts, make the explanations as to why something must be done in a particular way, and encourage those who are trying but not quite there. That means at times I can be long-winded and overly technical, at other times persuasive. I think my time as a sales assistant and the reading of Dale Carnegie's *How to Win Friends and Influence People* as a teenager helped dilute my teacherly ways.

The point is there is no one way to do the job; Cabinet is a team sport and a champion team is superior to a team of champions. While I never played team sports (which helps to explain why I was happier outside the factional system), I did feel comfortable with my role in Cabinet.

For government to work effectively all those diverse skills need to work together and all ministers have to take on whatever role their personality and skills equip them for. I was the 'Peacemaker'; Kevin 'Attack Dog', and Mike the 'Chief Salesman'.

§

It is in parliament, particularly during Question Time, where all these skills and attitudes are on display, where weaknesses are exposed and strengths rewarded.

The stated purpose of Question Time is for ministers to provide information to members about issues of the day, within their portfolio responsibilities. In reality Oppositions use it to set traps for ministers with the ultimate goal of getting a scalp. Governments use it to promote achievements and undermine shadow ministers. It's the place where the media, in particular, judge the relative strengths and weaknesses of key players.

For some members, Question Time is the part of the political process where they truly come into their own. Stephen Halliday, a long-term staffer and former chief of staff to Mike Rann in Opposition and government, commented to me in 1994 that the newly elected Kevin Foley was a potential Labor leader. I was astonished. I liked Kevin and we enjoyed social times together but he struck me as a young knock-about bloke with more ambition than talent. How wrong I was. Stephen made his evaluation about Kevin based on his performance in Question Time; he rated highly what he described as Kevin's 'natural authority'.

As Labor secretary at the time I didn't see much of Question Time. But when next able to I observed Kevin and understood what Stephen meant. Kevin was a natural; he looked confident, had strong and authoritative body language, and was a gifted and combative debater. On song, in both Opposition and government, there was none better than Kevin Foley. And he did scare and intimidate Opposition members. Sometimes, though, especially towards the end of his career, he could go too far and embarrass himself and the government. The following examples show the two sides.

PARLIAMENT

First, Kevin in answer to a question on the Budget on 15 September 2010:

> *In coming to office, we instituted in excess of $1 billion of Budget cuts in our first four years, from memory. We dragged the deficit into surplus. In doing so, within two years we were in receipt of an upgrade to a AAA credit rating, after two budgets. This government had done the hard work, had done the difficult work that members opposite ignored and refused to do because they were weak when it came to financial management ... We maintain a credit rating. We have done the hard work, and we will continue. Notwithstanding the yapping dog, the member for Norwood, back there with his raised eyebrow trying to outdo his colleagues in the front, I will say this, that we are a government proud of our financial record ...*

Second, Kevin on 29 October 2009 in answer to a question on probity:

> *Obviously the deputy leader – some would think shadow treasurer; of course I do not – is clearly afraid to ask me a question. I think I have had about two questions, if that, in my time here. I cannot recall a debate with the shadow finance minister on the radio, which I do every morning or every week –*

> *(Mitch Williams takes a point of order on relevance)*

> Kevin: 'Mr Speaker, I would just like to know, before the election, who to deal with when it comes to finance matters.'

> *(The Speaker tells Kevin to deal with the substance of the question.)*

> Kevin: 'You are the weakest shadow treasurer I have ever seen.'

> *(The Speaker calls 'Treasurer'; other members interject, he calls them to order too.)*

> Kevin: 'The weakest link ...'

The answer proceeded in this vein for some time with numerous interjections and calls by the Speaker for order, which were ignored. Eventually the Speaker said:

ON BEING A MINISTER

> *If I do not feel that I am able to control this chamber, if members continue to ignore my calls for order I will resign; I will go over to Government House and hand in my commission. The behaviour today has been nothing short of disgraceful and makes me ashamed to be a member of this place.*

That night's TV news was dominated by the uproar – once again reinforcing the view that the government was arrogant. Kevin may have undermined the shadow treasurer's confidence; but it came at a price.

Some ministers do not thrive in Question Time. My predecessor as health minister, Lea Stevens, a competent and caring person, just couldn't seem to make it work for her. Also a former teacher, Lea obviously knew a great deal about the issues and genuinely tried to answer the questions asked; however, she often seemed defensive and anxious.

Dean Brown, her shadow, often asked questions about particular problems for patients – usually relying on the fact the minister couldn't or wouldn't know the details and would have to get a report. This was a favoured approach by Brown and it was a tactic adopted from our term in Opposition – find a victim to illustrate whatever point you want to make about the health system or the education system. This was the approach Mike picked up from his mentor and friend Bob Carr, who had used it successfully in NSW as part of his campaign to win government. It's an approach designed to capture media attention and make the minister look out of touch and uncaring.

If you want to make the point that there is not enough support for children with disabilities in our schools it is made much more graphically if you can do it accompanied by a mother and a child in a wheelchair. I was determined, when I took over, to stop Dean Brown using that tactic on me.

In the media, just before I was appointed to the health ministry, I compared Dean to Colonel Klink in the 1960s TV series *Hogan's Heroes*. I claimed that 'he thinks he's running the show and thinks he's very important, but he's really just a comical figure'. It helped that Brown shared a similar owlish quality with the actor playing the hapless Klink.

In preparation for Question Time I asked my office to identify every potential 'victim' we could and set up a file for me so that if asked I could respond with more than a promise to get a report. This approach was more successful than I could have ever imagined; I struck gold in the very first week.

Just before my second Question Time as health minister my office had identified someone I might be asked about. Quick staff work meant I was able to get a report and ring the complainant, the widow of the 'victim'.

In Question Time, Dean on cue got the call and asked me about the case involving the treatment of a now deceased man at the Riverland Hospital.

I was able to tell the House:

I have also spoken to the widow ... The CE of the Riverland Hospital has made an arrangement to meet with her on Wednesday ... I have told her we will have an investigation into the matter. I apologised to her on behalf of the health system for what happened to her husband.

She congratulated me, by the way, on my appointment as the Minister for Health and wished me well. I said to her that, despite the facts she described in her letter and despite the fact her husband's circumstances were far less than ideal at that particular time, it was not a reflection on the entire health system. In fact, we have a very good health system in South Australia, and she agreed with me. In fact she said her husband had suffered with cancer and had been undergoing treatment for some six or seven years at the Royal Adelaide Hospital. She also said that if it had not been for the excellent treatment received at that hospital she would have been a widow some six or seven years earlier.

Brown had nowhere to go; his strategy of embarrassing the health minister by asking questions about individuals had been countered. My side was cheered; John Rau, then a backbencher, sent me a note: 'That is the *first time* that one of those questions from Dean has been answered well.' The next day the *Advertiser* reporter, former Victorian Liberal MP Craig Bilsteen, reported that 'refreshingly, Mr Hill confronted an appalling hospital stuff-up resulting in the death of a 69-year-old man head on – in stark contrast to the style of his predecessor'.

A couple of weeks later Dean Brown announced he was not going to contest the next election and stood down from the shadow ministry. Now, this was probably just coincidence, but I couldn't help think that my success in parliament had some bearing on his announcement. You make your own luck, I suppose.

I learned about good preparation for Question Time the hard way. Iain Evans, who before the change of government in 2002 had been the environment minister, became my shadow. Over the course of several months he asked me a series of low-key questions about radioactive waste storage. This had been an issue during the election campaign and was still a hot topic.

At the heart of the enquiries was the wish to ascertain if I received any recommendations on the issue. Generally, I answered that I wasn't aware of any such briefing – or words to that effect. Then on 24 March 2003 he asked me: 'Has the minister yet to receive a recommendation in relation to a low-level waste repository?' And I responded, 'The answer is no.' He knew he had me.

PARLIAMENT

A few days later Evans rose on a point of privilege and was able to reveal a briefing document prepared by the department and given to me. It stated: 'The establishment of a low-level radioactive waste repository is recommended by the Department of Human Services ...' He called for the independent Speaker, Peter Lewis, to 'rule on a *prima facie* case of breach of privilege in relation to misleading the house'; if the Speaker so ruled, then a Privileges' Committee would be set up to investigate whether I had in fact misled parliament. If I were found to have done so, I would have had to resign my commission.

With a different Speaker and a parliamentary majority this matter could have been resolved that day. My apology and an explanation to the House that I hadn't read the document in question would have been accepted by the majority. I would have been embarrassed and we would have moved on.

Unfortunately, on the day in question, the premier was absent and his staffers were making decisions on the fly and I ended up being locked into support of the very tribunal that could finish my career.

As it turned out, a Privileges' Committee eventually sat after a week of damaging speculation in the media; eventually, it and the House, did accept my explanation. For this I have Pat Conlon to thank. He was one of the members of the committee and he used his formidable skills as both a lawyer and waterside worker to have the committee deal with the matter in a sympathetic way.

I suffered the worst couple of weeks of my political life during this period and felt relief that it was over, gratitude to Pat and others who had supported me, and a determination to not let it happen again. I was also grateful to Kevin who was very supportive, as were many – but not all – of my colleagues. Kevin took pleasure in ringing me a month or so later to inform me that an approval poll to be published the following day showed I continued to enjoy high public support; proving once again that what obsesses politicians rarely makes an impact on the public.

I learned a lot from this episode, demonstrating the truth of the Nietzsche epithet: 'That which does not kill us makes us stronger.'

As I explained to the House, after the Privileges' Committee report was debated, the briefing note used by Evans was an attachment to one of 506 documents provided to me on becoming environment minister. Collectively, these briefing notes filled up several arch lever folders and ran to more than 1500 pages.

Whenever an election is held government departments prepare 'red' folders and 'blue' folders to hand to the incoming minister, depending on his or her political allegiance. Similar folders are prepared following reshuffles. The briefings give an overview of the department, issues, and an analysis of the new government's policies. And annoyingly, the Opposition had been supplied with a full set of the red documents by the department following an FOI request. Evans was canny enough and committed enough to work his way through the folders. He had only one job: to end my career. As a new minister I had a bit more on my plate. As I told the House 'it would be like giving someone a set of encyclopedias for Christmas and then 12 months later asking whether they had read a particular page'.

On becoming minister I had tried to work my way through these folders, but there were so many pages and issues I just put them to one side to get on with the job of governing – setting up an office, meeting key players, pushing the policy agenda. Little did I know that within these bureaucratic folders sat a 'time bomb'. When I was transferred into the health portfolio I told the department I didn't want the conventional briefing folders.

Instead I arranged for key individuals from the various parts of the agency to give me face-to-face briefings accompanied by a two-page briefing note. This was a much better approach – and while it took longer, it meant I was better briefed and there were no unread files to trip me up. I have recommended this approach to several new ministers.

The 'near death' experience also made my office sharper in its operations. Every question and answer was thoroughly checked; following the decision to live stream parliament this was often in real time. That meant I could quickly correct any mistakes, sometimes in Question Time itself. Under the protocols that govern ministerial behaviour a minister must not mislead parliament. Of course any deliberate misleading or lying is fatal: you have to resign your commission. During the Liberal Government's term we witnessed the resignations of several ministers: John Olsen in response to a report that he gave 'misleading, inaccurate and dishonest evidence' to an inquiry; Graham Ingerson for 'misleading parliament'; and Joan Hall following an auditor-general report that accused her of 'inventing evidence'.

Accidental 'misleadings' happen reasonably frequently; you misremember a date or fact, someone tells you something inaccurate, which you repeat. There are many ways to make errors. Kevin Foley, who could be extravagant in his claims on occasions, was very good at protecting himself from charges of misleading parliament. He would regularly start his answers with either the phrase 'I have been advised ...' or 'to the best of my knowledge ...' followed with 'I'll check the facts and if I have made an error I'll come back to the house'. A smart way for someone prone to shooting from the hip to protect himself. It's a good habit to adopt and I tried; but I also loved to use definitive yes and no answers.

When I did make mistakes, particularly with figures, I would come into the House, usually on the next day of sitting, and seek leave to make a ministerial statement. Within that statement I'd correct the record and often include additional information so that my corrections rarely looked like corrections. It's one thing to correct the record; it's another matter to draw attention to it. Of course, if the mistake were a 'whopper' I would make it clear I had been in error and apologise, as well as providing the correct information.

Question Time is a wonderful part of the Westminster system – it has a street-fight quality to it, which repels and fascinates voters in equal measure when they see the worst of it every night on their TV screens. It is not dignified, but it does test the mettle of the leadership teams on both sides. As I would tell visiting school groups, parliament is an adversarial system, where disputes are resolved by talking and voting, not by fighting. Symbolising this is a red line, known as the 'blood line', marking the floor before the frontbench desks on both sides. The space between, allegedly two sword lengths, is the means by which members are kept apart.

But it can be fraught. On one occasion when in Opposition I recall Kevin Foley in full combat mode having a go at the government. It aggravated the usually mild-mannered government whip and former private-school deputy principal John Meier so much that he crossed the 'blood line' with his fists raised; it was only the restraint of his colleagues that prevented him from laying into Kevin. This South Korean-style outburst was a rare exception.

My preparation for sitting weeks and Question Time was usually the same. Each Monday morning of sitting weeks I would meet with my key advisors to go through the week's agenda – focusing on issues that might be raised. Usually, it was pretty obvious what the Opposition was pursuing either because it was already a big issue in the media or it was something they had previously asked questions about. Then there were the issues we knew about, but we didn't know if the Opposition also knew about. So my staff would have briefing notes prepared on all these matters.

I usually took two folders with me in to Question Time: one for the health portfolio, and one for everything else. The health folder would have between 20 and 30 parliamentary briefing notes (PBNs); the second folder would have details of recent 'victims' – individuals who had made their criticisms about their treatment public in some way, or who had threatened to do so. This folder also contained briefings on arts and southern suburbs matters. I also liked to keep a set of key statistics on me – the number of hospital beds, waiting time averages and so on.

In the hour before Question Time on each day I would eat a sandwich and then go through the issues of the day with my key staff. This would mean checking our Dorothy Dixer; that is the question and answer prepared by my office for a backbencher to ask, usually highlighting some achievement or other. Sometimes we would use it to attack the Opposition over its claims. I would also use this time to make sure I understood the key issues on which I might be questioned. So I'd check on the PBNs to make sure I knew what they contained. In reality I knew that no matter how well we had prepared, when it came to the floor of the chamber it would be just me, the Opposition question, and my own fallible memory. Rarely, was the question such that the PBN could be read out as a complete answer. When it could, it was magic.

My approach to answering questions in parliament was the

same as it was with the media. Answer the question asked, with as many facts as possible, placed in the broadest possible policy context. Having a strong strategic policy framework allowed me to contextualise any question. If I were asked about waiting times at a particular hospital I would provide the overall system figures (which were good and improving), outline overall projects aimed at improving outcomes, and then deal with the specifics. Where possible I would finish by criticising the performance or lack of policy of the Opposition.

Here is an example from 5 September 2012; my response to a question from Martin Hamilton-Smith about 'ramping' at Flinders Medical Centre started with facts: 'In July 2012 the Flinders Medical Centre emergency department recorded 5978 presentations compared with 4995 in July the year before ...' I then provided great detail about the ED's performance showing that there had been a reduction in the amount of time the ED had 'high demand' status: 'the monthly average for July 2010 was 42.6 per cent, for July 2011 it was 12.6 per cent, and for July 2012 it was 6.7 per cent ...' More stats followed and eventually I went into teacher mode: 'What the hospitals try to do is to have a transfer of patients from the ambulance within certain set time frames ...' (Note: I didn't use the pejorative 'ramping'.) 'There is no policy to hold patients in ambulances outside the emergency department as there was prior to the recent changes at the hospital ...' Then, following some interjections, I finished by making a political point, somewhat pompously, that 'the interjections on the other side, of course, do not aid debate. What they do is just show that there is a competition on the other side for attention. We understand that ...'

To be honest I never felt entirely comfortable in Question Time – it's not my natural habitat, as it is for some members. Pat

Conlon, in particular, loved the opportunity to excoriate any Liberal who dared ask him a question. He was so confident that he would rarely bring in a briefing note, relying on his memory and superior debating skills. Kevin Foley, Mike Rann, and Mick Atkinson, as attorney-general, were also very effective in Question Time.

One's performance in Question Time is affected to a large degree by the person asking the question. Dean Brown would ask detailed questions about individual patients, Iain Evans would always try and set a trap. Other shadow ministers I faced, including Vickie Chapman, Duncan McFetridge and Martin Hamilton-Smith, were usually easier to deal with because they were more political in their approaches – they wanted to debate policy or performance.

For example the question asked by Hamilton-Smith about ramping referred to above: 'My question is to the Minister for Health. Has the minister's claim, made on 28 August, that no patients had been ramped in ambulances at Flinders Medical Centre since 16 July been proven inaccurate and, if so, what are the correct facts?' He then 'explained' that representatives of the nurses and ambulance unions had made claims that were contrary to mine.

Despite the attention it receives and the preparation it requires, Question Time is a relatively insignificant part of the parliamentary day. The average parliamentary week has 18.5 hours of sitting, of which Question Time takes up only three hours. There are a couple of hours for private members' time, with the rest of the time taken up by government business.

§

ON BEING A MINISTER

I once asked my mentor, Greg Crafter, if he had any regrets about his term as Minister for Education. Only one. Not enough legislation. Education has one main piece of legislation: the *Education Act*. Greg found that most of his policy agenda (for example ridding our schools of corporal punishment, and introducing promotion based on merit) could be achieved by administrative action. He felt that was an easier and faster way to make changes than by opening up the legislation and then being at the whim of every bit player in the Legislative Council who might want to trade their vote for a win in their own area of obsession.

This meant his key initiatives were vulnerable to a change of government. One such case involved the Education Review Unit, based on the UK's Her Majesty's Inspectorate, and set up to assess on a regular basis the performance of schools – particularly that of school leadership and teaching staff. Over time this would have driven school-based improvement via a thorough and public assessment of schools, leading to the removal of staff who were not performing. Regrettably and short-sightedly the incoming Liberal Government junked the project and used the resources to measure the performance of individual children. Not necessarily a bad thing in itself, but no substitute for a regular rigorous and public evaluation of how our schools are performing.

If Greg had wrapped legislation around this policy it is unlikely to have been scrapped. The conservative nature of the upper house can work both ways. I learned from his experience. Legislate, legislate, legislate!

Although I have a law degree I have never practised law – but I have made laws. From my point of view this is a far more thrilling experience than interpreting laws or challenging them in a courtroom.

As environment minister I knew I wouldn't have a lot of new money to apply to the issues, but I could write tough laws that would stand the test of time. I would say to environmental activists who argued for increased funding that a few dollars extra for environmental purposes was nothing compared to stronger laws.

In my four years as Minister for Environment and Conservation I introduced 24 Bills and numerous motions, expanding our national parks and wilderness areas, rewriting the laws across native vegetation, natural resource management, the River Murray, heritage protection, water conservation, dolphin protection, dog and cat management, waste management, and so on.

The most complex and extensive of the Bills I presented was the *Natural Resources Management Bill 2004* (NRM), which brought together community-based organisations separately dealing with water management, soil conservation, and animal and plant pest control. There were 60-plus distinct and overlapping bodies, with their own management and control and budget systems. These bodies were run by local individuals with strong community connections and views about how to proceed. The former government had wanted to reform this area too. In order to do this they proposed better coordination of the existing bodies by placing over them another layer of boards. Once again, afraid to take on vested interests in their own communities.

When I took the legislation to parliament it had gone through an extensive process of consultation with key groups such as the Farmers' Federation and Local Government Association, as well as members of existing boards. Most agreed with the general policy, but as always the devil was in the detail, much of which I addressed in extensive discussions over months and months of work.

The Bill took around 50 hours of debate to get through both houses of parliament and involved considerable amendment to even get it through my own house, where we relied on key country members such as Karlene Maywald from the Riverland, who when joining the government as the Minister for the River Murray ironically took responsibility for part of the legislation.

Karlene, in particular, was assiduous in her examination of the legislation and raised numerous objections, many of which I thought were nit-picking; all of which I tried to address and accommodate by means of amendments developed on the fly.

Eventually, the heavily amended Bill was forwarded to the Legislative Council where a similar process of 'worst case scenario' examination of every clause occurred. Eventually, my elegant, simple and straightforward piece of legislation emerged as something of a horse designed by a committee. A lot more complex than it needed to be and far more expensive to operate. But nonetheless it was through.

In my almost 11 years as a minister I introduced dozens of pieces of legislation that were passed by both houses, only once having to resort to a deadlock committee, the method of last resort to reach agreement between the two houses. However, a few Bills, which I judged had little hope of success, did lapse.

In order to get legislation through I would do as much groundwork as possible to get key lobby groups on side. It makes a big difference if the AMA, LGA, or nurses' union supports a measure.

Secondly I would make sure that all MPs, especially Opposition shadows and key crossbenchers in both houses, were well briefed.

Alex Keen had worked briefly in the office in an admin role. She was, unbeknownst to me, a lawyer who had worked interstate for a big property law firm before returning home to give government a go. Following the 2010 election I gained the mental health portfolio and was in need of a new advisor who could cover that policy area and who ideally had legal skills. Catherine Hockley, who was by then my chief of staff, suggested Alex, since Alex had worked on the new mental health legislation within the department. It took a little while to get used to the fact that the pleasant young woman who did the filing was now my mental health and legal expert.

One of Alex's many jobs was to look after my legislative program and in particular to brief Opposition and third party MPs. We always knew when Alex was briefing the Libs – she'd put on a nice frock and her pearls; this was not cynicism on her part but respect. Of course, she had them eating out of her hand.

As Minister for Environment I had been pleased that at the conclusion of the marathon House of Assembly debate of the NRM legislation the shadow minister Iain Evans had said: 'I thank the minister for the way the committee was handled. It was a difficult and long Bill, and I thought we handled it reasonably well in the circumstances. I also thank the minister's officers not only for their efforts over the last two days but also for the previous briefings given to me and my colleagues: we certainly appreciate that.'

With legislation I took the parliamentary process seriously and made myself available, especially to key independents in the upper house, who often felt taken for granted by government ministers.

I was surprised by the number of my lower house colleagues who didn't personally ask upper house independents directly for support on key pieces of legislation, relying instead on their upper house colleagues to do the work.

ON BEING A MINISTER

I always found the members of Family First, despite its very conservative morals agenda, easy to deal with. Generally, if I could mount a good case, Pastor Andrew Evans initially, and then Dennis Hood his successor as leader, would be as good as their word. Dennis would often let me know of his disappointment that he was supporting us but we never supported his measures. True. But unlike some other upper house independents, he never tried to trade his vote in exchange for government support for one of his measures.

I also listened carefully to Opposition objections. If I could accommodate them in the lower house, even when we had a majority, it would avoid the vengeance that would follow in the Legislative Council. Some ministers, such as Mick Atkinson, would never give an inch, relishing the lower house conflict and using every opportunity to bait the other side; I adopted the 'you catch more flies with honey' approach. Here is 'Atko', as he was known by all, interjecting on Isobel Redmond, on 25 March 2009, during debate on electoral reform:

> Redmond: 'I remember that, during the last election, the young Labor candidate was seen by one of my staffers to be taking down one of my corflutes. We contacted him and very politely pointed out to him that he might not be aware that that was an offence under the Act, but we were not going to take it any further –'
>
> Atkinson: 'Why don't you make the allegation outside without parliamentary privilege? Make it outside.'
>
> Redmond: 'I did; you can ask him ... if you talk to ... (him), you will find out that he did get a very polite and very nice phone call from us.'
>
> Atkinson: 'Well, he may have, but it may have been based on a falsehood.'
>
> Redmond: 'I can guarantee the Attorney that my PA ... was the person who saw him doing it.'

Atkinson: *'Yet another smear under parliamentary privilege. You have a reputation for it.'*

On 13 October the same year in answer to a question on motorcycle gangs Atko included the following information in his answer: 'Mr Speaker, this is a government whose ministers don't use words like "shit", "wanker" and "turd" live to radio. We are not the kind of government whose leader uses expressions like "vinegar stroke", "donkey punch" and ...'

Following the inevitable, but slow to arrive, 'point of order' Mick concluded with: 'All I can say is that the Leader of the Opposition and the shadow attorney-general have potty mouths like members of outlaw motorcycle gangs ...'

Atko stood down from the ministry following the 2010 election, and then in one of the best examples of poacher becoming gamekeeper was appointed Speaker in 2013 where, with humour and great knowledge, he proceeded to do an outstanding job lifting the standards of the House.

With the appointment of Stephen Wade to the position of shadow attorney-general the possibility of managing legislation smoothly came to a crashing halt. While I could often get Opposition support for a piece of legislation in the House of Assembly, when it went to the Legislative Council Wade would like to apply his very 'legalistic' mind to every measure. This at best caused serious delays and at worst meant important measures, where there was a general consensus, were threatened. Many ministers encountered this experience.

Some might say that it's great to see the Legislative Council assert its independence and exercise its traditional role as house of review; however, it meant that in dealing with the Opposition you could not rely on the shadow minister's view about their position. Heavens knows what a shambles this would be if they applied this approach in government.

§

I've long fantasised about reform of the Legislative Council. I would like to see it more like the House of Lords, on which it was based. In particular, it should have powers of review and delay but not rejection – like the House of Lords. And like the Lords, members should be part-timers who receive sitting fees only. My preference would be to increase its size to about 50 members, up from the current 22, all elected at each election for a four-year term (rather than the current eight-year terms) using a proportional representative system. This would mean huge diversity in representation – anyone who could get two per cent of the vote would win a place. This would create a large and broad community 'sounding board' for ideas and opinions, a kind of permanent 'focus group'. It would mean people outside the political class would be able to be heard. Of course, like the Lords, ministers could be appointed from among its members. This would make it easier for governments to appoint experts from outside the political mainstream to their Cabinets, in the way a British PM or US president can.

One of my failed pieces of legislation – the Public Park Bill – was the most political. It was designed to wedge the Opposition. The Bill was aimed at creating a public park over the Crown land in the state's central north, which the Howard Government had identified for use as a national radioactive waste facility. In order to advance this, the Howard Government needed to compulsorily acquire the land. The Cabinet was advised that we had the power, through legislation, to create a 'public park' over the land and by that means prevent Commonwealth acquisition;

Commonwealth legislation prevented acquisition of land in a 'public park' without state government consent. A neat way of blocking the Feds.

The legislation was introduced in the upper house, where predictably the Liberals and a number of crossbenchers, including Terry Cameron, former Labor member and my predecessor as Labor secretary, voted it down. While this was disappointing, our resolve resonated with a broader community very much opposed to the Commonwealth move. Rann got the politics absolutely right. The public like to see their government fight for something. Our approach infuriated the national government, which only saw the rationality of its case. When governments ignore community feelings and attitudes, develop a 'tin ear' as Simon Crean said of Julia Gillard, you know they are in deep trouble.

Despite this loss we had another string to our bow, which was to argue our case through the courts where, surprising everyone, we were successful and the Commonwealth backed off.

10
PERSONAL

*Nobody on his deathbed ever said,
'I wish I had spent more time at the office.'*
Attributed to Paul Tsongas (1941–1997), US Senator

In 1987, in the months before our November wedding day, Andrea and I went in search of our ideal home. We had a clear idea of what we wanted: an inner suburb, ideally Goodwood, which was close to friends and had a cosmopolitan ambience we liked. We wanted open fires, a cellar and garden, and room for Andrea's two little boys and us.

We looked at dozens of houses during that period, experiencing a mixture of excitement and frustration as we surveyed the best of what we could afford. We marvelled at the small cottage that had a full-scale church organ crammed into a front room but been emptied of everything else including floorboards and ceiling. We laughed at the larger house where every room was filled with kitsch pastel plastic decorations. And we put an offer on an exquisite art deco house in Toorak Gardens, but without success. We were starting to get a little anxious, until one Saturday, when flying home from an interstate ministerial meeting with my boss Greg Crafter, I glanced through the real-estate section of the complimentary *Advertiser* and found the house in Goodwood; our new home.

It had everything we wanted and more – a two-minute walk

for the kids to Goody Primary, it was close to shops, tram, train and open space. It had a lovely garden with roses and fruit trees and lawn and a big cedar tree in which I built the kids a tree house. Eventually, we renovated the house to make it even more comfortable and in line with our needs.

We loved that house and the lifestyle we developed there; the kids brought their friends around for sleepovers; we enjoyed dinner parties with their parents and other mates; and in September we walked down the road to the Royal Show.

In 1989 I stopped working for Greg Crafter and became a Labor Party organiser, a quaint title reflecting the modelling of the Party's organisation on that of unions. In practice, my job was to do whatever the state secretary, Terry Cameron, wanted. Trades Hall was a five-minute drive from home; and I was now in the machine that would eventually deliver a seat in parliament to me, as it had done for nearly every one of my predecessors.

But when and how and where?

Over the 1991/92 Christmas/New Year holiday break I took a call from Cameron suggesting I consider putting my hat in the ring for Kaurna, a newly created seat on the southern outskirts of the city. About as far from Goodwood as you could be and still call yourself an Adelaide resident. The electorate (Baudin) on which Kaurna was based was being vacated by long-term MP and former deputy premier Don Hopgood, who had resigned his commission at the same time as the former premier John Bannon.

Cameron stipulated one condition: I had to move into the electorate. A good thing too; how else can one properly represent a community? MPs need to know about local schools and hospitals and roads and buses by using them, not by visiting them.

Andrea knew I wanted to go into parliament and we had briefly discussed an opportunity in the northern suburbs, which we both dismissed. I had also rejected, in my own mind, any thought of going to Canberra. I admire those who serve in the national parliament; but having recently married I didn't want to sleep in any bed at night other than the one in my own home. Too many Canberra marriages fall apart, or so I thought.

I was up for the challenge of Kaurna, despite there being only a nominal 3.5 per cent margin and the State Bank collapse being the defining issue. As Tim Stanley, who at the time was talked about as a future premier and who became a Supreme Court judge, said to me: 'If you win Kaurna, you'll be set for life.' I agreed and decided to give it the best shot possible.

Andrea, selflessly and with deep regret, agreed to move from our home and community to an area neither of us really knew. Once again the house hunting began; what became plain was that the available houses were much cheaper (a good thing) but they seemed pretty small. It took us a long time to find a home in Seaford that suited us.

The preselections were in January 1992 and we moved to Seaford in July that year. That meant big changes for everyone. We decided that Luke, in year 9 at Adelaide High, would continue there and commute each day with me. I was still working at the Labor Party office in Trades Hall and as I liked to get to work by eight o'clock that meant we left home around 7.15; it also meant Luke was generally the first kid to arrive at school. It was a good thing he was an avid reader. I felt bad, especially in winter leaving him on the school's doorstep waiting for someone to open up, with only his paperback for company. But he never complained and it meant that for more than three years we spent almost two hours in each other's company on most days. We quickly resolved the issue of what radio station to listen to; I preferred ABC Classic and he Triple J – so in the morning my choice prevailed and his in the evening. They were long days for him – but leavened by the shared burden of the commute and the pleasure of learning about each other's musical taste. There was one announcer on Triple J who used to make both of us laugh – a good way to end the day.

But for Luke, living in the south never worked and as he moved through school his friends and interests were more and more on the other side of town. It came as no surprise, but nonetheless an emotional shock, when he decided to leave home in his second year at uni.

For Eric, who was only ten, commuting to Goodwood, despite his desire to do so, was never an option. In the mid-year break we enrolled him at Moana Primary where he quickly made friends. Eric soon enough became a real 'southie' and played both cricket and football for local teams. Saturdays became a balancing act for me between transporting Eric, watching him play, and door knocking.

Eric eventually went to Seaford 6–12 School, among the first intake of students. He had some good teachers and he and his closest mate, Chris, did pretty well. Despite this, at the parent night at the end of Year 10, when senior courses and what they led to were discussed with all of the Year 10 parents, no mention was made of preparing for university entrance. Not for Eric; not for anyone. As a middle-class university graduate and former teacher I was astonished; even now 16 or so years later the memory of it rankles. Andrea and I, of course, asked the teacher running the evening about this omission and he told us that it was not necessary as most people only aspired to TAFE courses.

Of course, he had a point – very few local school leavers did go to university; but it was hardly helped by the narrow expectation shown by the school. Low expectations and a paucity of experiences seemed to be a common factor in our community back then. On one occasion when Andrea was driving Eric and a friend somewhere Eric talked about some of the countries he wanted to visit. Andrea asked the other boy where he wanted to go. 'Nowhere, travelling is for wankers.' Another boy came around at dinnertime and Andrea asked him if he would like some soup. 'What's soup?'

As Minister for the Southern Suburbs I did a lot of work on a policy I called 'Clever Communities'; the idea was to work with local leaders – in sport, schools, community, business – to lift expectations about academic achievement of mainstream kids. Unfortunately, available funding went into an admittedly worthwhile but narrower program targeting school dropouts.

In Eric's case, Andrea, he and I worked through what he needed to matriculate and made sure he did. He was lucky to have an exceptionally good English teacher who helped him master academic writing. At one stage, Eric felt pressure from his peers, some of whom were bringing in what seemed like a good income, while he was still at school. Both Andrea and I told him he could leave school if he wanted, we wouldn't object. His response was telling and made the point about family expectations better than I ever could. Eric said, 'How could I not go to uni when my mother has a PhD, my brother a LLB, and my father is an MP?'

Eric did matriculate and went to the University of Adelaide, as his brother before him. Both boys graduated with two degrees, including law. Both were invited to join the Golden Key International Honour Society, offered to students who achieved grade point averages putting them in the top 15 per cent of their disciplines. To say Andrea and I were proud of them both is like saying Homer Simpson enjoys beer.

Eric's and Luke's successes prove to me something that I have long believed: unless the principal of the school is cruel or mad it doesn't really matter which school kids go to – what matters most is what the family puts in. The really exceptional schools are the ones that can give kids what some parents are either incapable of or unwilling to provide.

For Andrea moving south meant big changes too. Kids can adapt pretty quickly, but it's harder as an adult to make all the links and connections that make you feel you belong in a community. Andrea, like countless spouses of police officers, school principals, bank managers and so on, coped magnificently.

In the mid '90s Andrea's parents moved nearby and other family members followed. We become involved in local groups and got to know people. What was unfamiliar became familiar.

Now, after leaving our house in Seaford, at 22 years the longest either of us has lived in any one spot, we are nostalgic about what became our home – the garden, the beach, coffees in McLaren Vale, walks in the Onkaparinga National Park, the clean air and open skies.

§

While moving home 23 years ago was difficult, what was really tough on Andrea was my absence. As a candidate from the beginning of 1992 until the election at the end of 1993 I threw myself into campaigning. Starting early I would doorknock all day Saturday and Sunday, public holidays and other 'days off' until nightfall. Then most nights I would be out at community events: Neighbourhood Watch meetings, school council meetings, sporting club presentations, amateur theatre groups – you name it; where two or more constituents were gathered together you would find the Labor candidate for Kaurna – and often the Liberal candidate too. After losing the 1993 election there was very little respite as I became Party secretary and soon again candidate for Kaurna, where I put in even more effort to make sure I didn't lose a second time.

These were very hard years for Andrea – I was never home when it was light and when I did make it I was often exhausted or needed to do follow-up work associated with my visits. All this as the boys went through their teenage years. I don't think I realised until my election loss in 1993 how my campaigning affected my sons – I had been optimistic about winning, but in my heart I think I knew my optimism was misplaced; so I was in a sense prepared for what happened. But I didn't really think about how it would affect Luke and Eric; after getting the results, I returned home for the 'wake'. Both our boys were sitting in front of the election broadcast with tears in their eyes. They were devastated.

But both of them played important roles in subsequent victories, as did Andrea. In 1997, Luke was 18 and able to vote and I ran an ad in the local paper with a letter to young people explaining why he was voting for 'his dad'; it was accompanied by a photo I'd snapped of him one morning in his pyjamas – he had a big smile and uncombed long hair. It was real. Even the then Federal Liberal MP, Susan Jeanes, said her daughter had seen it and was impressed by this attractive young man. By the 2002 election, Eric had turned 18 and I re-ran, in a pamphlet, the same style ad. Eric puts down the big swing I received at that election to his contribution – he claimed, probably truthfully, that he knew by then just about every young person in the electorate.

In my 1997 victory I had used a handwritten letter from Andrea to the women in Kaurna saying why she thought I'd be a good member. I was astonished how this simple message stood out against the dozens of messages bombarding electors.

As tough as it was on the family, from a campaigning point

of view, the hours I committed to meeting people was the correct approach – I won comfortably in 1997 and saw my majority strengthen in 2002 and then again in 2006; although I suffered a big drop in 2010, the early work (I doorknocked most homes in the electorate at least three times before I was elected) had lasting benefit. As a minister I had much less face-to-face contact with electors but constituents contacting my electorate office would often say to staff that they knew me, based on a house call up to fifteen years earlier.

As a former Party official I've always taken an interest in campaigning techniques and how they help win votes. I've seen direct mail, the 'hero' pamphlet, telephone canvassing, street corner meetings, and the developing use of social media. I followed Obama on Twitter and was astonished during the Obama–Romney contest when I received a direct tweet from Michelle Obama telling me to 'Be the difference in this election'. A little difficult from Australia!

All these techniques can help but nothing beats face-to-face canvassing at the front door. People remember it and it helps them believe you are real and seriously want their vote. Mind you it doesn't work if you are a jerk; I went doorknocking once with a candidate who, as soon as the voter opened the door, would regale them with a list of his qualifications and his opinions. He lost.

Not only did Andrea not have my company, she and the boys had to put up with rumours, and abusive and demanding phone calls. When we first arrived in the south a rumour was circulated by members of the Liberal Party that Andrea was one of the richest women in Adelaide. We had no idea why or how that rumour started; it certainly wasn't true. When we met, Andrea had been recently widowed and was living in a shabby rental house.

Our home phone number was also the campaign phone number and the more I campaigned the more people called and, of course, Andrea and our sons would answer the calls. And while most people were fine and just wanted information or help some were aggressive or weird; one bloke regularly rang when he was drunk and one woman rang on Good Friday advocating capital punishment. Any political candidate will tell similar stories. But the straw that broke the camel's back as far as I was concerned was the pathetic individual who tore into 14-year-old Luke, swearing at him and threatening him and me with physical violence. After that the phone was always on answer machine mode – for the next 20 years I filtered every phone call made to our home line. Not only has it cut out these sundry ratbags and time wasters, but we also avoid all those phone calls from mobile phone providers.

What it couldn't filter out was an out-of-control local boy and his friends. This lad was a little older than our kids and seemed to take an instant dislike to my family and me. At various times we had to put up with verbal abuse, loud music, spitting, egging, beer and cigarettes thrown on our car, urinating against the fence and then, the coup de grace: a middle-of-the-night fire in our wheelie bin pushed up against our brush fence. His parents told us he didn't like politicians, Asians (we have relatives with a Malaysian background) and 'home boys' (a reference to our middle-class kids, I guess). The late-night fire was particularly disturbing and if it hadn't been for Andrea's sense of smell, the fence and potentially our house and lives could have been affected. As it was we had only a broken night's sleep, a melted bin and a visit from the fire brigade. A week later the bin was set alight again, with the same outcome. We talked to the police, who were helpful, but as there was little evidence there wasn't much they could do. Eventually we replaced the brush fence with a metal one and we had probably the only house in Seaford with an external fire alarm,

Eventually, after years of aggression, this too passed. In fact, late one night coming back from parliament I saw the boy hitchhiking home and decided to give him a lift. He was by then a bit older and he confided in me that he suffered from a mental illness and was sorry for the grief he had caused.

When I became a minister the nature of my reasons for not being at home changed but the hours didn't. If anything, initially at least, I was out for even more hours. Paul, my driver, would collect me at 7.10 am, get me to the office around 8 am and then take me home when all the meetings, speeches, events, receptions and dinners were over; this could be midnight or later.

As environment minister, in particular, I was often very busy on weekends, visiting country locations to meet with the incredibly committed volunteer groups who work in our parks or along our waterways. My responsibilities in the arts portfolio meant many nights and weekends taken up attending events – usually very pleasantly.

The invitations to many of these events and dinners came with 'and spouse' attached. Andrea gave great service and accompanied me to a huge number of 'functions' (one of her least favourite words). Arts events were usually enjoyable but the formal dinners can be a bit of an ordeal, even when their purpose, such as raising funds to combat some childhood disease or other, is noble. Inevitably, the dinner's progress is punctuated by speeches, auctions and entertainment. Terrific if it's something you go to once a year, but when it's weekly, well ...

§

There are ministers in governments all around the country who are single, who seem to be able to do their jobs well. I don't know how; I just know that without the support and love of my wife and children, I would never have achieved anything in politics. Ironically the first time Andrea became aware of me was in a political context – in 1982, when as the candidate for Mitcham my pamphlet went into her letterbox. She remembers thinking at the time – this guy looks OK, but what he needs is a wife and a couple of kids. Little did she realise then that within five years she would be supplying me with all three.

Not only was I nourished by Andrea's love and supported by her presence, I was also able to exploit her history and connections in country SA. At various times as a child Andrea and her family lived in the Barossa, the Riverland and Woomera, and her grandmother died and was buried in Port Lincoln. When I visited the Angaston Hospital I was able to stand in the room where Andrea was born; in Lyrup I could point to the main street, 'Wilson Street', named after Andrea's father's family, who were part of the original white settlement. I think local communities appreciated that this 'suit' from the city had some connection, no matter how tenuous, to their district.

Only years later did we discover that an early direct ancestor, Joao (aka 'Runaway Portuguese Jack') Antonio, who arrived in Adelaide in 1837 on the *Sarah and Elizabeth*, owned property around Morphett Vale and was buried in the grounds of St Mary's Catholic Church on South Road at Morphett Vale. A campaigning tool unexploited!

The longer I served as a minister the better I became at achieving some sense of work–life balance. Instead of leaving home at 7.10 am every day I would leave an hour before my first appointment and try to keep at least one day on the weekend free. And Andrea instituted a rule – optimally, no more than two nights out in a row, for her.

One habit we maintained through my ministry years was to take holidays; a couple of weeks in summer, usually spent at home, and two weeks in winter, usually spent somewhere warm: Darwin, Cairns, Noosa, Broome. The warmth was always a welcome reprieve from cold Adelaide winters; but we also enjoyed the relative anonymity that came from being away from home – though that was never assured. I will never forget the occasion when on a driving holiday in New Zealand I was lobbied at a roadside stop by a woman who worked in amateur theatre in Adelaide.

I was fortunate in the areas of responsibility I had as a minister – environment, health and arts. From each of these areas I learned a lot and on a personal level had my life changed by my exposure to the ideas and people working within each field.

I was disappointed to have been given the environment portfolio as a shadow minister – I thought it was relatively small beer and I wasn't really interested in the issues. But I was determined to make it work. Andrea, of course, was delighted – she was a committed environmentalist in her domestic life. She recycled, composted, emptied pots of water from the kitchen on the garden, and religiously turned off lights. I was a bit of scoffer; but was converted by the job. And when Mike Rann offered to give me something else as we moved towards government I asked to hold onto it. There were things that I now felt passionate about and wanted to achieve in government.

And I changed my behaviour. In particular I learned to love

being outside. Once I was that Leunig character watching a sunrise on TV; now I prefer the real thing. In particular I began to garden. For years I watched as Andrea, with great joy, looked after our garden; participating, only, with objections, to do some of the heavier jobs she couldn't manage. But suddenly, I got it and, of course, in that annoying way alpha males have, became the expert at pruning and mulching and feeding. I cannot think of anything that gives more pleasure; and to our joint delight it is something we can do together.

While I have always enjoyed the arts, other than the study of literature as part of my arts degree, I have no real knowledge. Spending 11 years as a minister, exposed to the finest this state can offer and being able to talk with those who have knowledge and expertise, has been an incredible education. Who knew that I'd enjoy opera, including Wagner, so much? Or contemporary Asian culture? Or Patricia Picinnini? Or indeed produce and sell four pieces of 'art' for charity auctions?

§

We all know the *Yes Minister* parody of the education minister who is illiterate, the unfit sports minister ... and the unhealthy health minister.

As a minister if you are really to be convincing in your job you have to walk the talk. It would be challenging for a chain-smoking junk-food consumer to be health minister. I had stopped smoking decades before I became health minister, and I exercised regularly at the gym and gardened, but I did eat and drink too much. I am lucky to enjoy very good health, which I assume I have inherited from my mother, an active 98-year-old, rather than my father who died soon after his 59th birthday. But I was overweight.

PERSONAL

Over the years I gained weight and then, with huge effort, would lose it – only to see it slowly return. In about 2008 I decided to make a major change to reduce weight and keep it off permanently. I put myself on a low-carb diet, as proposed by the CSIRO. And it worked and worked quickly, within six months I went from 87 kilograms to about 72. I felt great and now, seven years later, I have managed to keep most of the weight off. I am healthier now, in my 60s, than I was in my 40s.

The public response was interesting; friends and strangers alike would sidle up to me and in that particular way people have when they expect bad news would say, 'Are you all right?' There was speculation in the media that I was seriously ill and certain members of Caucus, anticipating a vacancy, became very interested in my health. Finally, the premier took me to one side to ask if I was all right. In the end, in an address to a business lunch, I raised the issue in a speech dealing with obesity. I argued we had become such over-consumers of calories we had normalised obesity and that when someone lost weight and developed a healthy BMI, we perversely thought they were ill.

People would also say of me that I always seemed calm – in the media and in meetings, regardless of the political problems and pressures I was facing. And it is certainly true that when faced with pressure I don't panic, and in some ways relish the challenge of working through complex issues in a logical and determined way. I seem to convey those qualities in person and in the media. Good qualities to have, no doubt, for a person in public life. The media and the public love nothing better than to see someone in public life lose control, throw a tantrum, or break down in some way; it's not a great career move to be thought of as tempestuous, emotional or flaky. Just ask Mark Latham.

However, as is often the case, the public man is not always the private man, and I am ashamed to say that too often Andrea and my boys saw my worst side. At home I could be angry, intolerant, emotional or, worst of all, silent. Not always, but often enough to know I could hurt those whom I love most. I have often sought to understand this. If I had lost it more at work would I have been a better husband and father? Was I really just an actor pretending to be calm in public? Or was I a control freak, who once the public eye was removed could let it rip?

My bet is that at work I was in charge; I had staff to do my bidding, not in a servile way, but willingly because they trusted and believed in me. I had authority and status. I was an important person. I was also the oldest son of an angry and remote man, whose love and approval I could never quite feel; here was my opportunity to get that love and attention on a grand scale. At home I was just another member of that great democracy: the family. My words were questioned, my decisions ignored. I wasn't in charge. Instead I was loved and I sometimes used the protection of that love to let the veneer slip, to let the dark angel's wings flutter from time to time.

Now, at the end of my political career, my only regret is the bad deal my family got. My great solace is that they stuck with me and I feel fiercely bonded to them, as they to me.

When I first met Andrea I was already working in politics full-time. I told her politics is what I am. Her requests that I consider other careers were answered with what I thought of as a truism: I am a politician in my core in the same way an artist is an artist. I have to pursue politics. And I have for over 30 years. Now that I have left the ministry and contemplate a future beyond politics I know that fire has been extinguished. I have no more political ambitions left. I will always follow the political caravan's travels, but I won't any longer be in the wagon. It feels good.

AFTERWORD

Nearly all men can stand adversity, but if you want to test a man's character, give him power.
Abraham Lincoln (1809–1865), 16th US President

All citizens have power – it will vary depending on wealth, health, geography, intelligence, appearance, family, education and luck. But we each can make decisions about our lives to a greater or lesser extent. I am talking about the power we exercise in our daily lives in relation to our family, friends, jobs, hobbies, holidays and the like.

But, it seems to me, we also each have a kind of reserve political power. It's the power exhibited in protest movements, mass demonstrations, civil disobedience, revolutions. When individuals come together to shout 'no more!'.

Normally, citizens only exercise of that power is every three or four years at the ballot box when they delegate their 'reserve' power to us, their political representatives. When they make their choice to lend that power to one party or another they want it to be exercised in their interests; they don't want it to be sat on. Paul Keating, reflecting on his time as prime minister, was riveting as he stared down the barrel of the camera waving his bony index finger, expounding on the nature of such power. Governments have political capital, which they have to use; like any capital – if it's not invested it will lose value.

Citizens want governments to use their power – though they will object if it intrudes too far into their personal space. Unless, as in the case of tobacco control or road safety, governments can make a compelling case for such intrusion.

The challenge for government is to work out how to spend that capital in a coherent way in the overall interests of the community. The role of ministers is to bring forth the options and then be part of the process of determining priorities and implementing them. A group of intelligent and united people with brave leadership and clear and consistent values should be able to make it work. At least that's the theory. Of course, leaders are not always brave, ministers are not all intelligent, and often they are not united.

Ministerial positions are not advertised, there are no minimum education requirements or necessary relevant experiences, references from previous employers are not checked, and there are no interview panels. Once appointed there is no induction program, in-service training, or career counselling. From the moment you are sworn in by vice-regal authority the training wheels are kicked away and (to mix the metaphor) you have to sink or swim under your own steam (to mix it again). And you have to do this while the Opposition, media, public service, and your own party, fellow ministers and the community, scrutinise every detail. Every error is pounced upon, while most achievements are ignored or attributed to others. Why would you bother? Well, it's the most thrilling job you can have, though this is not a view commonly held. All through my career people would come up to me, introduce themselves, comment on how I was going as a minister and say, 'I wouldn't do your job for anything!'

To be any kind of success in the job you need to know what it is you are trying to achieve and to be deliberate about it. The late

AFTERWORD

Frank Blevins, a former Labor deputy premier, was briefly, in the early 1990s, Minister for Health – not a job he wanted or intended to keep. He was in a holding pattern until a new minister was appointed, so knowing he was to be there for only a limited time he fine-tuned his goal for health and chose a neglected issue he felt strongly about. As a result of his efforts South Australia has the nation's best pregnancy advice clinic operating out of its own premises, where women and girls can receive accurate advice and abortions if required.

As a minister you need to hire quality, hard-working staff who will tell you when you are wrong and then take a bullet for you when you are. You need to establish an open, trusting and productive working relationship with your chief executive and if you can't, get rid of him or her immediately and find someone you can work with.

Then it's a matter of working hard without procrastination, dealing with the issues as they arise in an open and decisive way, and communicating with colleagues, and the community, parliament and media as fully as possible.

Be brave, have fun, and make your own luck.

THANKS

To my first readers for their intelligent and helpful suggestions

Andrea Dale, Ruth Awbery, Dominic Stefanson and Clem Macintyre

INDEX

2GB 108
5AA 108, 117

A
Abbott, Tony xii, xiii, 36, 69, 94, 120, 148
ABC radio/television 6, 39, 104, 106
Abraham, Matthew 104–108, 115
Adams, Brer 5, 78
Adelaide Festival 80
Adelaide Review 117
Adelaide Symphony Orchestra 81
Adey, Paul 2, 27, 130
Advertiser 6, 11, 14, 60, 69, 109, 110, 111, 114, 115, 126, 127, 168, 184
AMA. *See* Australian Medical Association
Archer, Robyn 81
Armitage, Michael 75
Artarmon Public School 146
Askin, Robert x
Asquith Boys' High School 84
Atkinson, Michael 175, 180
Australian (newspaper) 117, 119
Australian Medical Association (AMA) 51, 60, 67, 97
Awbery, Ruth 13, 30, 103, 110, 118

B
Baggoley, Chris 124, 126
Bailleu, Ted 161
Baluch, Joy 81
Bannon, John (and Bannon Government) x, 1, 26, 110, 148, 185
Berri Hospital 123
Bevan, David 104–108
Bilsteen, Craig 168
Birch, Jim 34, 124
Bjelke-Peterson x
Blevins, Frank 201
Bligh, Anna 131
Bolte, Henry x
Borys, Jean-Michel 76–78
Bottrall, Jill 98
Bracks, Steve 161
BreastScreen SA 133
Bressington, Anne 20
Breuer, Lyn 19, 154
Brinkworth, Tom 11–12
Brown, Dean 56, 74, 166, 168, 175
Brown, Steve 80
Buckett, Kevin 126
Bush, George 93
Button, James 85
Byner, Leon 108, 117

C
Cain, Chris 51, 60

Cairns, Jim   131
Cameron, Terry   183
Carr, Bob   166
Ceruto, John   110
Channel 7   111, 116
Channel 9   97, 111
Chantelois, Michelle   154
Chapman, Vickie   46, 51, 96, 113, 175
Chifley, Ben   ix
Christley, Stephen   103
Ciccarello, Vini   19
Clinton, Bill   xiv, xv, 85, 93
Coetzee, J.M.   102
Colonel Klink   167
Commonwealth Parliamentary Association   154
Conlon, Pat   xvii, 5, 37, 39, 54, 130, 151, 161, 169, 175
Conroy's Smallgoods   125
Corcoran, Des   114
Country Health Plan   68
Court, Charles   x
Crafter, Greg   1, 17, 22, 26, 34, 38, 176, 184, 185
'Crazy John'   113
Crean, Simon   183
creative federalism   xiii

D
Dale, Andrea   3, 87, 122, 154, 184–196, 198
Dale, Eric   116, 187–190
Dale, Luke   186–192
Davidson, Tony   117
'debate and decide'   64, 70, 75, 152
Debelle Report   139

Department of Water, Land and Biodiversity   xiv, 37
Dog Fence Board   42
Dorothy Dixer   173
Dunstan, Don   x, xi, xiii, 5, 22, 89, 110

E
EPODE   76, 77, 78
Evans, Andrew   180
Evans, Iain   2, 37, 38, 168, 175, 179

F
Family First   180
Farrell, Don   10
Farshid, Gelarah   137
Federation   ix
'Festival state'   80
Finks Motorcycle Club   160
Flinders Centre for Cancer Innovation   87
Flinders Medical Centre   141, 174
Flinders Medical Foundation Annual Ball   87
Florida, Richard   80
Foley, Kevin   36, 37, 54, 57, 151, 152, 155, 164, 171, 172, 175
Fox, Chloe   79
Fraser, Malcolm   38, 59
Freeman, Rob   xiv, 55
Fringe Festival   80

G
Gardiner, Phil   65
Gaydar   127
Gerard, Rob   65
GFC. *See* Global Financial Crisis (GFC)

INDEX

Gillard, Julia xvi, 69, 94, 119, 148, 158, 183
Gillies, Max 51
Global Financial Crisis (GFC) xi, 45, 49
glossophobia 84
GP Plus Healthcare Centres 67
Gray, Gary 92, 96
Griffiths, Steven 96
Gunn, Graham 32, 45

H

Haikerwal, Mukesh 51
Halliday, Stephen 6, 164
Hallion, Jim 36
Halton, Jane 36
Hamilton-Smith, Martin 60, 105, 112, 121, 140, 174, 175
Hawke, Bob 90, 93
Hayden, Bill 9
Health Advisory Councils 75
Health Care Act 2008 76
Health Care Plan 68
Hewitt, Brendon 48
Hewson, John 95
Hill, Aaron 10
Hill, Jack (father) 86, 92
Hill, John
  and awkward photographs 112, 113, 115
  Arts policy 79
  backflips 21
  bans plastic bags 82
  Beauvais visit 78
  called 'Minister' 7
  candidate for Mitcham 114
  Centre-Left faction 9
  'clean desk' strategy 17–18, 26–27
  comes to South Australia x
  compromise in politics 53
  cooking and staff lunches 15
  dealing with electors' problems 21–23
  decision making 26–29
  defamation case 116
  delegation of authority xv, 55
  doorknocking 95, 189, 191
  environmental salt remediation 11
  family members. *See* listings under 'Dale'
  first ministerial portfolio 1
  first speech 84
  first visit to ministerial office 3
  fitness and health 197
  fluoridation in Mt Gambier 20
  former teacher 163
  grandparents 92
  idealism 52
  law background 9, 147, 176
  learning media management 6, 14
  learns tactical voting 146
  leaves office xvii, 153
  long tenure in office xvi–xvii
  member for Kaurna 9, 185, 186, 190
  Minister for Environment and Conservation xiv, 177, 179
  Minister for the Southern Suburbs 188
  Ministerial Council, chair 27
  'misleading the house' 169
  move to Goodwood 184
  move to Seaford 186
  necessary bureaucracy 19, 23, 24–25
  non factional stance 8, 151, 154
  nuisance complaints 22
  parliamentary driver 2–3
  'Peacemaker' 163

reform of the Legislative
  Council   182
sets up ministerial office   4
'Team Hill'   15
time in Opposition   53
TV, use of   92–94
uses iPad   30
visits Montreal   65
visits Norway   65
Hill, Kathleen (sister)   92
Hill, Moira (mother)   87, 92
Hockley, Catherine   6, 11, 12, 13, 78, 106, 127, 179
Holloway, Paul   10, 53
Holmes, Allan   4, 38–39, 40
Hood, Dennis   180
Hook, Rod   39, 40
Hopgood, Don   185
Howard, John   93, 95, 117
Hudson, Hugh   149
Hunt, Paul   8

I
InDaily   40
Ingerson, Graham   171

J
Jackson-Nelson, Marjorie   61
James Nash House   47
Jeanes, Susan   190
Jones, Alan   108

K
Katsaros, Jim   65, 67
Keating, Paul   ix, 38, 89, 92, 95, 199
Keen, Alex   178
Keith Hospital   71
Kelton, Greg   69, 96, 111–113
Kennett, Jeff   xiii, 161
Kenyon, Tom   122

Kerin, Rob   12, 156
kidney transplant services   67
King, Cathie   4
King, Len   5
Kitselaar, Amy   30
Kotz, Dorothy   129
Koutsantonis, Tom   154

L
Lakoff, George   100
Latham, Mark   197
Latty, Yvette   6
Lee, Carolyn   3–4
Leitch, Kelvin   146
Lewis, Peter   147, 169
Listeria outbreak   125
Lomax-Smith, Jane   8, 121
Lyell McEwin Hospital   xvi, 97, 103

M
Mackie, Greg   100
Malinauskas, Peter   157
Mansell, Mel   60, 110
Manuel, Leah   15, 121
'Marj Mahal'   62
Marjorie Jackson-Nelson Hospital   60. *See also* Royal Adelaide Hospital (RAH)
Marshall, Steven   10, 121
Maywald, Karlene   123, 147, 178
McEwan, Rory   147
McEwin, Lyell   xvi, xvii
McFetridge, Duncan   175
McTernan, John   72, 119
'Media Mike'   94, 159
Meier, John   172

INDEX

Menadue, John 58
Menzies, Robert ix
Millhouse, Robin 114
Minchin, Nick 147
Modbury Hospital 69
'Mr Teflon' 112
Mt Gambier 20, 21, 74
Murray, Andrew 104

N
Nemer case 99
Nixon, Richard 93
'nocebo' effect 162

O
Obama, Barak 85, 93, 191
O'Brien, Kerry 147
Olsen, John 37, 94, 95, 129, 156, 171
OPAL 76, 77

P
'Painters and Doctors Union' 51
Panter, David 41, 45, 46, 59, 64
parliamentary briefing notes 173
Pearson, Christopher 117–119
Perryman, Steve 21
Picton, Chris 10, 13, 54
Pisoni, David 77
Playford, Tom x, xvi, 161
Port Augusta 81
Portolesi, Grace 139, 140
Pow, Deb 3, 6
Public Private Partnership (PPP) 144

Q
Queen Elizabeth Hospital xvi, 60–61, 67, 68

Question Time 164, 166, 167, 168, 171, 172, 173, 174, 175

R
radioactive waste dump 98
RAH. *See* Royal Adelaide Hospital
Rann, Mike xi, xvii, 1, 2, 6, 8, 35, 53, 56, 57, 59, 78, 94, 98, 99, 100, 108, 111, 117, 118, 120, 121, 131, 148, 151, 153, 156, 159, 160, 164, 175, 183, 195
Rau, John 154, 155, 156, 162, 168
Reagan, Ronald xv, 1, 55, 56, 85, 93
Redmond, Isobel 45, 63, 77, 88, 96, 112, 121, 180
Regional Centre of Culture 81, 82
Reid, Alex 7
Reid, George 102
Richardson, Graham 63
Richardson, Tom 40, 97, 111
Richter, Jenny 59
Rodda, Rachel 86
Rodney, Vic 15
Roxon, Nicola 10, 36, 54
Royal Adelaide Hospital (RAH) 29, 41, 44, 46, 49, 54, 57, 60–68, 110, 125, 145
Rudd Kevin xii, xiii, xv, 45, 69, 86, 94, 129, 158
Ryan, Des 110

S
SA Health Care Plan 59
SASMOA. *See* South Australian Salaried Medical Officers Association
'Save the RAH' team 65

Scanlon, John   37
Sherbon, Tony   7, 13, 34, 42, 44, 45, 106, 132
Shine, John   44
Shine-Young Report   45
'shock jock'   108
Simcoe, Anthony   93
'Sir Humphries'   32
Smithson, Mike   111
Snelling, Jack   39, 64, 70, 134, 138, 155, 156, 157
Snowtown (film)   79
South Australian Health and Medical Research Institute (SAHMRI)   44
South Australian Salaried Medical Officers Association SASMOA   103
Southcott, Heather   114
speeches, speechwriting   85–90
Spring, Geoff   36
Stanley, Fiona   61
Stanley, Tim   186
State Bank of South Australia   x, 186
State-Federal power   x–xiii
Stefanson, Dominic   24, 137
Steinle, John   17
Stepping Up report   47
Steptoe and Son   19
Stevens, Lea   56, 166
Stone, John   38
Sunday Mail   65
Sutton, Evan   84
Swan, David   7, 35, 103
Swan, Wayne   10

T
Talbot, Nick   5, 11, 43, 98
Thatcher, Margaret   53
Thinkers in Residence   xi, 72
Thomas, Kath   16
Today Tonight   116
Tonkin, David   114
Treasury   33, 36, 38, 46, 47, 48, 49, 50, 58, 82, 143, 156
Twitter   120–122

W
Wade, Stephen   181
Wangarry bushfire   130
Weatherill, Jay   xvii, 2, 10, 33, 40, 50, 52, 64, 78, 120, 140, 152, 155, 156, 160
Whitlam, Gough   ix, xvi, 59, 89, 131
Williams, Mitch   12, 165
Wilson, Mavis   3
Winter-Dewhirst, Kym   1–3, 5
WomAdelaide   80
Women's and Children's Hospital   63, 64, 67
Worth, Robert   114
Wotton, David   4
Wright, Jack   149
Wright, Jim   49

X
Xenophon Nick   20, 21

Y
The Year My Politics Broke   69
Young, Alan   87

§

Supreme Federalist
The political life of Sir John Downer
J.C. Bannon

Supreme Federalist exposes the intricacies of politics at the time of Australia's transition from the colonial era to the modern federal nation. Sir John Downer (1843–1915), founder of a political dynasty, combined strong conservative values with a liberal approach; championing legal reform, the advancement of the rights of women and children, and opposing the White Australia Policy.

Praise for *Supreme Federalist*
'A balanced and fresh perspective on Australia's political transformation from a group of colonies to a modern federal nation.'
– Nic Klaasen, *Flinders Ranges Research*

'As a political family history, this is an extraordinarily fine book.'
– Rama Gaind, *PS News*.

ISBN 978 1 86254 835 0

For more information visit www.wakefieldpress.com.au

DON DUNSTAN
Intimacy and Liberty
Dino Hodge

Don Dunstan, Premier of South Australia in the late 1960s and throughout the 1970s, is acknowledged as one of Australia's foremost civil rights advocates of the twentieth century. He actively promoted the rights of Indigenous Australians and women, and he passionately pursued multiculturalism. More than any other political leader in the country's history, Dunstan championed the rights of homosexual citizens at a time when they were treated as criminals, classified as insane, and regarded as outcasts. He was also bisexual.

This book records the change in public discourse over issues of homosexuality – from morality to state security and then civil liberties. Dunstan worked as a member of parliament for more than twenty-five years, and then throughout the remainder of his life, to realise his vision of full equality for same-sex attracted citizens. He focused on both legislative and cultural reforms, and introduced changes to the Police Force that were unprecedented and strongly resisted. His efforts and the backlash he suffered are fully documented here for the first time, finally giving due recognition to one of the country's most remarkable champions of human rights.

Praise for *Don Dunstan: Intimacy and Liberty*

'This book will inform teaching and research across a broad canvas of Australian history. I commend it as both intellectually compelling and thoroughly enjoyable.' – Barbara Baird, *Australian Historical Studies*

'The biography has been much needed to reveal more clearly the outstanding achievements of the Dunstan era and the special humanity of the man himself.' – Maggie Tate, *Global Media Post*

ISBN 978 1 74305 296 9 [Also available in ebook formats]

For more information visit www.wakefieldpress.com.au

Wakefield Press is an independent publishing and
distribution company based in Adelaide, South Australia.
We love good stories and publish beautiful books.
To see our full range of books, please visit our website at
wakefieldpress.com.au
where all titles are available for purchase.
To keep up with our latest releases, news and events,
subscribe to our monthly newsletter.

Find us!

Facebook: facebook.com/wakefield.press
Twitter: twitter.com/wakefieldpress
Instagram: instagram.com/wakefieldpress

www.ingramcontent.com/pod-product-compliance
Lightning Source LLC
Chambersburg PA
CBHW052049220426
43663CB00012B/2496